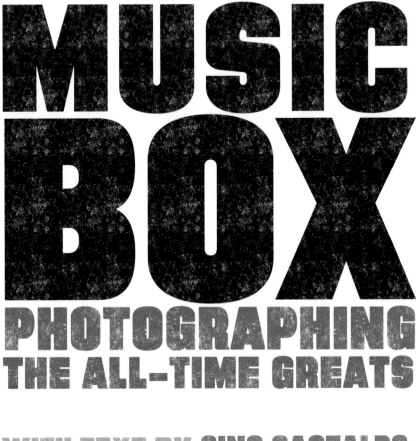

MUSIC BOX

PHOTOGRAPHING
THE ALL-TIME GREATS

WITH TEXT BY GINO CASTALDO

Thames & Hudson

Translated from the Italian *Music:Box* by Grace Crerar-Bromelow

First published in the United Kingdom in 2011 by
Thames & Hudson Ltd, 181A High Holborn, London WC1V 7QX

British Library Cataloguing-in-Publication Data
A catalogue record for this book is available
from the British Library

ISBN 978-0-500-51600-3

Printed and bound in China

CONTENTS

Freddie Mercury, Queen NEAL PRESTON, 1986

IMAGINING MUSIC

A **SINGER STANDS AT** the microphone, head up, eyes lost in the spotlights, hair streaming out behind. In the background the neck of a guitar points heavenwards and smoke wreathes around the stage. The photographer's eye has caught this exact moment, fixed it all in an instant that will remain forever, silent, immobile, yet enduringly linked to the music that lives in our memories. What's more, a skilful photographer can go beyond capturing this frozen moment. Where words fail, a photograph can reveal and express the uncanny essence of music. As well we all know, music is not just something we hear, we see it, too.

The real question is: could the blue touchpaper of rock 'n' roll have stayed lit without the iconic images that accompanied the sounds? Just think of Bill Haley and his kiss-curl. He had already recorded the catchy 'Rock Around the Clock' with the Comets in 1954, but the song wouldn't become a a hit until it was chosen to be played over the opening credits of *Blackboard Jungle* (1955), a film about delinquent teenage behaviour. It was precisely this projection of rebellious youth that excited disenfranchised young people across America and Europe. Images of James Dean and Marlon Brando – the faces of the new counterculture – had the same effect, and rebellious youth eagerly consumed the new visual fare.

A few years later, Elvis was taking various different elements of American music and weaving them together with his own original magic, but it wasn't until the people of the States had seen him on television that they took any real notice. And then they didn't just take notice, they were transfixed. The King held their astonished attention, as it dawned on them that a new page of world culture was being written before their very eyes. And it was everything to do with image. Presley's act was also his body: he had a bold face with (like Dean) an androgynous look, all topped off with that rebellious quiff; but, above all, it was the way he shook his legs that set the crowds screaming. You had to see it to understand.

Throughout the twentieth century, music has always needed image as a necessary complement to its intangible, transitory nature. And long before the advent of MTV and the music video, photographers had been capturing the smoke signals of flaming guitars, the raw defiance of smashed instruments, the intense features of jazz performers engraved by the music itself, the hairstyles, the gloom or excitement of backstage rooms and the ecstasy of an audience. If one placed all the most important pictures relating to music in one imaginary, infinite library, it would tell the story of the last hundred years, beat by breath by blow.

Perhaps it is true that in order to really understand music we must also be able to see it. After all, for thousands of years of cultural evolution music existed undisturbed in, and only in, its moment of creation. Music was always performance, and sound was inseparable from the direct visual relationship between player, listener and place. For this reason there was no need for any additional images, or for recreations or representations of the event. But once the phonograph had been invented in the late 1870s, it became possible to recreate a musical moment at will, beyond the natural existence of its immediate performance. It could be reproduced at any time – any number of times – for audiences anywhere in the world. The first and most obvious consequence was that from this moment on music, dislocated from performance, began to need images.

For the last hundred years, as technologies have appeared that make art reproducible, music has been interwoven with the image – each nourishing, changing and enhancing the other. Music has moulded and revolutionized symbolism in the graphic arts, and it has created whole photographic genres. Photography in turn has helped to define the world of jazz, with smoke, crowded clubs and the sly gleam of brass under basement lights. If recording removed music from its natural visual context, then a substitute is needed: either an album cover, a poster, a T-shirt: any touchstone or totem that will restore the visual integrity of music. These images remind us that no matter how many times a song was mastered, or how many records were pressed, it was once live.

Image was not only a substitute for 'being there'. It was also utilized as part of the careful creation of star quality. Frank Sinatra's first audiences were teenagers excited by the combination of an irresistible voice with the face of an Italian charmer. His blue eyes looking out from under a narrow-brimmed hat at a jaunty angle marked him out as both street-wise and smooth. The Beatles' supreme position as the band of the sixties was at least in part due to their arrival coinciding perfectly with the explosion of popular visual culture in Western society. Furthermore, their rise to fame – caught on magazine covers, in photos and in films – gives us a detailed account of how dizzyingly quickly celebrity images became ubiquitous and took over our lives. And since then we have been overwhelmed by stars whose dress sense draws attention, and also helps to define their musical style. David Bowie, for example, conjured up astonishing metamorphoses, using clothes to illustrate his various personalities and in doing so told a story that added another layer to his music. It's impossible to think of gothic music without dark garments; punk without studs and slashes; or glam rock without skin-tight outfits and glittering sequins: the attitudes of entire musical genres are defined by their visual style.

Photographs have captured singers at the emotional height of their songs; have described their iridescent hairstyles; have examined their faces and masks with a relentless curiosity; have contributed to the cults and myths surrounding some artists; have revealed mesmerized audiences; and have helped created unique looks. For example, it's impossible to imagine Madonna outside the visual spectacle that pervades her live shows and music videos. She plays the part of an icon; centering her performances around image, rather than the creation of a musical event. This lesson has been well learned by many of her imitators, who have also scaled the heights of the music industry using a seamless amalgam of music and images.

If music videos and film clips played over the television networks and the internet exist to describe a musical event, photography has taken up quite another, more challenging, role. The 'disadvantages' that separate still imagery from the moving picture have actually worked to its advantage. Photography is silent and it is instantaneous, capturing only what is to be seen when the shutter opens; freezing a single moment that might otherwise be lost among a million others. The beauty of a freeze-frame is that it puts the moment into the imagination of the viewer, leaving them to imagine a before and an after. For many, these timeless moments can come to stand for something greater, and, like the greatest music stars, become iconic. In an industry where the true greats have often lived fast, and died young, these brilliant instants begin to serve as metaphors, as well as images.

So photos have helped us imagine music in many ways since sound was first phonographically reproduced. At first it was simply a record of the face that made the music, then an attempt to bear witness to the moment in which the music was made. Next it became a shared intimacy with the stars, and after that it became one of the ingredients that helped create stars. It has been, along with the music, a tool of expression, and self-definition. And all along it has been art. Photography has brought an extra sense, colour, vision, depth and understanding to the modern experience of enjoying music. In doing so the two have become a fruitful and inseparable pairing in this, the greatest age of the image. How can we resist when the world's best photographers tell us the story of music?

Bruce Springsteen ANNIE LEIBOVITZ, 1984

WHILE MY GUITAR GENTLY WEEPS

**I look at the world and I notice it's turning / While my guitar gently weeps /
With every mistake we must surely be learning / Still my guitar gently weeps**

The Beatles

The Edge and Bono, U2
MARCELO DEL POZO, 2010

SIX THIN SHINY STRINGS, just six, all tuned to harmonize together in infinite combinations that have created lifetimes of music. In the right hands a guitar can produce jangling chords or pizzicato arpeggios, imitate percussion instruments or provide a dance rhythm. When electrically amplified, their energy can make whole buildings rattle and shake.

Above all, the reason for the guitar's huge success lies in its pleasing combination of shapes: the space that opens up in the acoustic version (the rosette), the long neck and the curves of its body that are so pleasing to hold. The instrument is so delightfully full of harmonies, melodies and rhythms, but also so compact that it can easily be slung on your back. It was one of the first nomadic instruments, an upstart vagabond.

The guitar, in one traditional form or another, has been with us for a long time, each varying design created and adapted to suit regional conditions. The international family of stringed instruments (including the lute, the sitar and the *guqin*) has already been used to create a great body of work, whether it be composing serenades below shuttered windows,

Muddy Waters TERRY CRYER, 1958

Kora player and rapper Omar
DAVID ALAN HARVEY, 2006

Robert Fripp
ANDY FREEBERG, 1986

aiding ancient prayers, driving away spirits or helping Orpheus to enchant all living things. Its greatest appeal to more recent civilizations in history was the ease with which it could be transported, accompanying minstrels and troubadours as they travelled, taking ballads and songs of romance from city to city.

Subsequently the guitar retreated to the background, and was played mainly in dance bands. It was not very loud, and not easy to hear when mixed up with other sounds (despite experiments with electric amplification that had been attempted in the 1930s and 40s). It was, however, the preferred instrument of the blues, a perennial complement to the laments from the Lower Mississippi, and in the 1940s Woody Guthrie toured New York with a guitar and tales of the Dust Bowl. But what turned the guitar into an icon, a myth, a mighty symbol? That took rock 'n' roll.

What was especially striking about Elvis, and many other stars of the rockabilly period, was that they had begun to wield their guitars like a sensual extension of their own bodies. This was especially the case with Chuck Berry: his instrument wasn't just there for

James Taylor
LYNN GOLDSMITH, 1980

Thurston Moore, Sonic Youth
NEALE SMITH, 2007

accompaniment, it was something quite different and menacing, more like a gun than a guitar. Berry live was a true showman, and wrote many riffs that defined his era. It was rock music such as 'Johnny B. Goode' that made the electric guitar both an absolutely key instrument and a dazzling symbol. The fact that it was the loudest thing in the room also helped it whip up the temperature.

The 1960s saw the boom of the guitar, and it soon became one of the most popular instruments. As huge quantities of cheap models flooded onto the market they also quickly became of the most democratic, so affordable that nearly every young Hendrix-in-waiting could get their hands on one. Once at home, their stiff little fingers ineptly picked out chords, or attempted to recreate the ostentatious rock riffs that had started to echo around the world. So music began to be played in millions of homes where previously it had been absent.

During the 1960s and 70s the influence of the electric guitar spread and the instrument became even more fundamentally important, progressing from symbol of rebellion to the

Eric Clapton DERICK A. THOMAS, 1989

Thom Yorke, Radiohead
ALESSIO PIZZICANNELLA, 2003

Charlie Christian
F. DRIGGS COLLECTION, 1940

voice of established culture. The Beatles used it to weave dream-like stories, Pink Floyd used it to carve sound into grand sculptures and Pete Townshend smashed his in a breathtaking frenzy. Eric Clapton, Jimmy Page and Jeff Beck turned the guitar (and the act of playing it) into the essence of style, while for Carlos Santana it seemed something more akin to a spiritual rite. There was a moment when the electric guitar seemed to be the most powerful musical weapon ever created. Jimi Hendrix, on that pale dawn on the fourth day of the Woodstock Festival, even used it to depict the very sounds of warfare, devastating the American national anthem and transforming it into the noise of aerial bombing in Vietnam. Some instruments even become sacred, untouchable, such as the one that belonged to Django Reinhardt. His Selmer guitar is preserved by the Manouche jazz musicians, who are convinced that it should never be played by anyone else as the sound died with the man who created it.

WOODY GUTHRIE

'This land is your land, this land is my land', sang Woody Guthrie in 1940. For the migrant, who had joined the hordes of other desperate workers in the 1930s, as they left their homes in the Central and Southern Plains of the United States to look for work in the the Promised Land of California, his words reflected the experience of dust, hunger and the long, hard road. This journey was an odyssey through the misery of the shanty towns, through the violence perpetrated by industrialists and the injustices inflicted by the authorities. But the Great Depression had found its bard. Guthrie, who had travelled as a migrant himself, said: 'I write what I see, I write what I've seen, I write things that I just hope to see. Somewhere farther along.' His music became a means of direct communication and protest in a way which was entirely new.

In the 1940s Guthrie's political engagement became ever stronger, but his most powerful weapon for change remained the machine that 'Kills Fascists': his guitar. He played with Pete Seeger and his Almanac Singers at trade union gatherings and political rallies, and he recorded albums of ballads about significant figures in American history, such as *Ballads of Sacco & Vanzetti* in 1947. Guthrie contrasted a country of affluent citizens and oil tycoons with the America of Ludlow, a company town where workers' families often lived in poor conditions. On the track 'Ludlow Massacre', he sang of a 1914 strike by the workers that was put down by the Colorado National Guard, resulting in 19 deaths.

Woody liked to think of himself as a worker rather than an intellectual, but he was to became a beacon to the younger generation of folk revivalists in Greenwich Village. For Bob Dylan, Guthrie was the absolute master, inspiration and guide, leading Dylan to write 'Song to Woody' when Guthrie was confined to hospital for many years with Huntington's disease. A 19-year-old Dylan went to visit his idol and sang him the verses he had written: 'Hey, Woody Guthrie, but I know that you know / All the things I'm sayin', and many times more / I'm singin' every song, but I can't sing enough / Cause there's not many men done the things that you done. / Here's to Cisco and Sonny and Leadbelly, too / And to all the good people that traveled with you/ Here's to the hearts and the hands of the men / That come with the dust and are gone with the wind.'

Previous pages **Ronnie Wood of The Rolling Stones** TERRY O'NEILL, 1975

Woody Guthrie ARCHIVIO GBB, 1943

Jean-Baptiste Reinhardt *alias* **Django Reinhardt** WILLIAM GOTTLIEB, 1940

B.B. King HOOKS BROTHERS STUDIO MEMPHIS, 1949

ROBERT JOHNSON

Heavy drinker, womanizer, hell-raiser. Robert Johnson, with his mysterious life, early death and diabolic mastery of his guitar, was born to be a blues legend. When he died at the age of 27 (tales of his poisoning are rife but unsubstantiated) he left only 29 tracks, recorded in 1936 and 1937. These were enough, however, to influence generations of guitarists.

Legend tells that, at a crossroads in Mississippi at midnight, Johnson had made a pact with the Devil: that he had sold his soul in exchange for the ability to play the guitar like no one else in the world. He helped to shape his own myth with the devastating poetry of his lyrics: 'I got to keep movin' / Blues fallin' down like hail / And the days keeps on worryin' me / There's a hellhound on my trail', he sang in 'Hellhound on My Trail'.

His incredible technique and innovative style, so instinctive and primitive, made him a musician for all time, and a luminary for more than just blues artists. Among those who count themselves inspired by Johnson were The Rolling Stones, who arranged a version of his 'Love in Vain'; and Cream, who covered his 'Cross Road Blues'. Eric Clapton said: 'Robert Johnson is the most important blues musician who ever lived...I have never found anything more deeply soulful. His music remains the most powerful cry that I think you can find in the human voice.'

Robert Johnson A PHOTOBOOTH SELF-PORTRAIT FROM THE EARLY 1930S

Elvis Presley ALBUM, 1956

Mike McCready, Pearl Jam ALESSIO PIZZICANNELLA, 2006

Prince HENRIETTA BUTLER, 1992

Joe Cocker STILLS, 1969

Buddy Guy GUIDO HARARI, 1994

Johnny Cash JIM MARSHALL, 1969

Carlos Santana MICHAEL OCHS ARCHIVES, 1970

LED ZEPPELIN

Led Zeppelin was beyond doubt the greatest rock band of the 1970s, and Jimmy Page, who founded the band with Robert Plant, was probably the most inspired and impressive guitarist of the era. The Led Zeppelin live show was an almost orgiastic aural experience, in which frequent musical experimentation, extended guitar solos, laser shows and pyrotechnics combined with the band's savage fury to hold the audience spellbound. Between 1970 and 1980 they made over 20 tours, often playing sets that lasted several hours.

When Page was just 13 he was given an old Spanish guitar: 'It was sitting around our living room for weeks and weeks', he recalls, 'I wasn't interested. Then I heard a couple of records that really turned me on, the main one being Elvis's 'Baby, Let's Play House', and I wanted to play it.' Electric guitars came on the scene sometime later. Some of Pages's favourites were the Fender Telecaster Paisley (played on Led Zeppelin's first album), the legendary Les Paul Standard and the famous double-necked Gibson, which was used for performances of the famous solo on 'Stairway to Heaven'.

Jimmy Page responded to criticism about his lack of precision and sloppy technique by saying: 'Technique doesn't come into it. I deal in emotions.' From the moans which he produced by playing the guitar with a violin bow in 'Dazed and Confused', to his magisterial improvised solo in 'Heartbreaker' and his powerful strumming alternating with arpeggios in 'Babe, I'm Gonna Leave You', it was Page's experiments that characterized the sound of Led Zeppelin. As Bryan May of Queen said: 'He's one of the great brains of rock music.'

Jimmy Page, Led Zeppelin TERRY O'NEILL, 1977

Jeff Beck GUY LE QUERREC, 2003

Patti Smith BILL KING, 1975

JIMI HENDRIX

The crowd at the Monterey Pop Festival on 18 June 1967 held its breath. Jimi Hendrix, back then still virtually unknown in America, was on next. And he had to follow The Who.

Pete Townshend had just left the same stage after having smashed up his Fender guitar in a show of ferocity that had the audience in ecstasies. Hendrix, worried that he might be eclipsed, took to the stage and 45 minutes into his set, during the pounding music of 'Wild Thing', knelt over his guitar, sprinkled it with a lighter fluid and set it alight in a public and psychedelic voodoo ritual. This rite of possession established his feral stage presence and the performance entered the annals of rock history. 'Those times I burned my guitar it was like a sacrifice. We all burn the things we love. I love my guitar.'

This wild dandy of rock 'n' roll was soon recognized as the greatest of all electric guitar players. Hendrix's solos borrowed influences from everywhere: rock and jazz, blues and funk. His improvisations were sometimes rough and scratchy, sometimes gently passionate, but he redefined the very nature of the rock guitar. Carlos Santana commented: 'He would really control that instrument like a jazz player or a blues player would. It was like controlling a demon and making it sing.'

Hendrix died young, and is noted as one of the five members of the '27 Club': a group of artists (including Brian Jones, Janis Joplin, Jim Morrison and Kurt Cobain) who all passed away at the age of 27.

Following pages **John McLaughlin** BOB WILLOUGHBY, 1992

Jimi Hendrix ED CARAEFF, 1967

Ramones MAX VADUKUL, 1977

Pat Metheny GUIDO HARARI, 1993

John Frusciante, Red Hot Chili Peppers GUIDO HARARI, 1999

Eddie Van Halen GUIDO HARARI, 1982

Jack White, The White Stripes ALBA TULL, 2008

Pete Townshend, The Who GRAHAM WILTSHIRE, 1975

BRUCE
SPRINGSTEEN

The November 1990 issue of *Rolling Stone* was a special edition in homage to the 1980s. On the cover the indisputable headline read: 'Bruce Springsteen: Voice of the Decade'. Springsteen wrote beautiful songs and filled whole stadiums, but his talent ran deep enough to defy his own inherent contradictions: he called himself 'a tramp born to run', but was commercially successful as a pop star; he spoke of the man in the street, of America's conflicts and its sins, and yet *Born in the USA* was celebrated as a galvanizing hymn to the American Dream; his image is that of the wholesome boy next door, but he become a rock icon. Now, despite his fame, the voice of the eighties gives the impression that he could happily go back to his old life in New Jersey at any time.

Springsteen's renowned live concerts often last for more than three hours, and when Dave Marsh, his official biographer, asked him why the performances were so long, the Boss replied: 'It's like you have to go the whole way because…that's what keeps everything real. It all ties in with the records and the values, the morality of the records. There's a certain morality of the show and it's very strict.' 'Nice guys finish last', concluded Marsh in a cover article for *Rolling Stone* in August 1978, 'and here's one at the top. So what's the catch? I just don't know.'

Following pages **Madonna** BOGDAN CRISTEL, 2009

Bruce Springsteen MARCELO DEL POZO, 2009

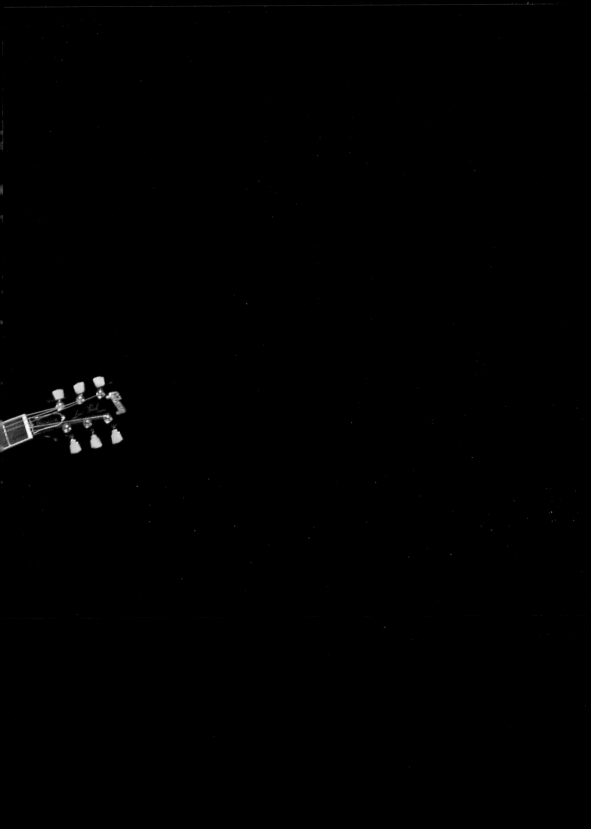

The Edge, U2 PARAMOUNT PICTURES, 1988

Paul Weller, The Jam PENNIE SMITH, 1977

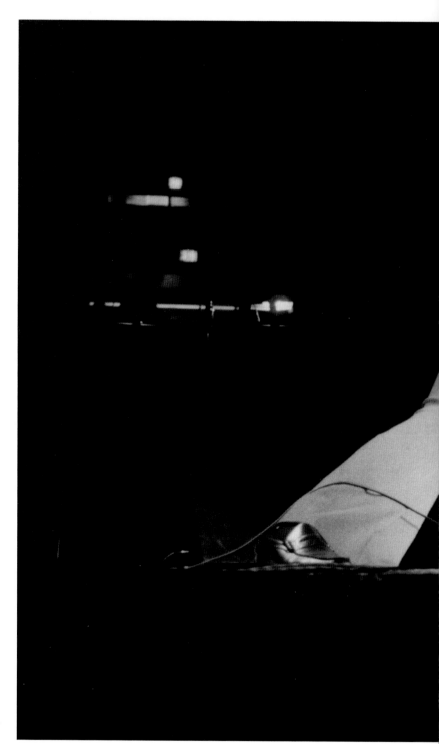

Chuck Berry
MICHAEL OCHS ARCHIVES, 1975

KURT COBAIN

When Nirvana's single 'Smells like Teen Spirit' came out in 1991, it was immediately clear that something in rock music, and in the spirit of the time, was changing. The lyrics were hailed as a hymn to a generation, whose official spokesman it was felt Kurt Cobain had become. But Nirvana's skinny lead singer was never comfortable with this role. Perhaps because, for whatever reason, that very 'teen spirit' seemed to him to stink to high heaven.

The album *Nevermind* seemed to sum up a cultural moment; it marked the end of one era in rock music and the start of another. It was a return to the sounds of the 1960s and 70s, there were no more synthesizers or keyboards, there was just a simple trio of bass, guitar and drums, but the angrily shouted choruses of their songs no longer suggested any of the utopian or liberating rebellions of those former years.

The band sang about the frustrations of life, depression, about a revolt without hope. The drugs weren't helping any more to open 'doors', although they did help with the pain. Kurt Cobain wrote in a note before killing himself at the age of 27 in 1994: 'I haven't felt the excitement of listening to as well as creating music along with reading and writing for too many years now. I feel guilty beyond words about these things. For example when we're backstage and the lights go out and the manic roar of the crowds begins, it doesn't affect me the way in which it did for Freddie Mercury, who seemed to love, relish in the love and adoration from the crowd which is something I totally admire and envy. The fact is, I can't fool you, any one of you. It simply isn't fair to you or me. The worst crime I can think of would be to rip people off by faking it and pretending as if I'm having 100% fun. Sometimes I feel as if I should have a punch-in time clock before I walk out on stage.'

Following pages **Ritchie Blackmore, Deep Purple** FIN COSTELLO, 1974

Kurt Cobain, Nirvana JEFF DAVEY, 1991

PETE SEEGER

Can you change the world with a song? Pete Seeger always thought so, because music can be reciprocated. The voice of one man can become the voice of many, and the voice of the many can be the voice of just one.

Like Woody Guthrie's guitar, Seeger's banjo was an instrument of protest, a fighting machine as well as a means of creating art. He inscribed on its exterior: 'This machine surrounds hate and forces it to surrender.' Together with Guthrie, Pete Seeger gave a voice to the music of his land; he sang the songs of the workers, and carried a message of unity and support for the oppressed to every corner of America.

Though blacklisted during the McCarthy era, he went on to become one of the greatest writers of protest songs in the 1950s and 60s. As well as penning one of the first anti-Vietnam War songs ('Waist Deep in the Big Muddy') Seeger also popularized 'We Shall Overcome', a tune that would swiftly become a folk and civil rights anthem. Many of Seeger's songs would later be reworked and reinterpreted by other artists, for example 'Where Have All The Flowers Gone?' has subsequently been sung by Joan Baez, Marlene Dietrich and Olivia Newton-John, among others.

Annie Leibovitz photographed this patriarch of American musical history on the banks of his beloved Hudson River, near Seeger's home in Beacon, New York. She took the picture during the Clearwater Revival, a festival of music and ecology that collects funds for the Hudson River Sloop, an environmental organization founded by Seeger at the end of the 60s. The father of folk music was standing on the bank in orange overalls, banjo slung over one shoulder, gazing towards the place where he had swum in the river as a child.

Pete Seeger ANNIE LEIBOVITZ, 2001

Bob Dylan ELLIOTT LANDY, 1968

YOU CAN LEAVE YOUR HAT ON

Baby, take off your coat, real slow / Baby, take off your shoes, here, I'll take your shoes / Baby, take off your dress / Yes, yes, yes / You can leave your hat on Joe Cocker

James Brown

HATS ARE SPECIAL: of the many accoutrements and accessories that mankind chooses to wear, none is more visible, or more characterising. Headwear can frame the face and hide (or accentuate) those windows of the soul – the eyes.

Just as soon as an artist dons a hat, they have sent out a strong message and – in one way or another – engaged in an act of self-definition. From king to fool the hat is an integral aspect of the uniform of rank and purpose, and the fact that it can be put on or plucked off, even swapped, must be liberating for musicians playing a new role in every song.

But which to pick? In music, where originality is crucial, repeating another's style – being old hat – would be a cardinal sin. This desire to be unique has led to artists favouring headgear of every conceivable style, almost like a contest of creativity.

Thelonious Monk's bearskins and trilbies were a symbol of his own mocking self-awareness, worn as an invisible smile; Elton John's hats became part of his audacious transgender style; Boy George's lent his androgynous look a sly edge; while, for Maurice Chevalier and Leonard Cohen, a hat was essentially a sign of good manners and respect for their audiences. By doffing them, the pair could create a supremely gracious moment.

The narrow-brimmed panamas worn by Frank Sinatra or Dean Martin were more than just a smart jaunty gimmick, they combined authority and poise. Lester Young's summed up his whole style, so much so that Charles Mingus immortalized it in 'Goodbye Pork Pie Hat' one of his most beautiful compositions. The cap that held Bob Marley's dreadlocks had religious

Boy George MARK C. O'FLAHERTY, 2001

Thelonious Monk GUY LE QUERREC, 1964

Bob Marley LYNN GOLDSMITH, 1980

significance by association; while the Blues Brothers' hats were such a trademark that they were virtually part of the brothers' bodies, only removed three times in total during the 1980 film *The Blues Brothers*.

In this long parade of hats made famous through their affiliation with musicians, we can see arabesques of carnival style, explosions of feathers, brightly coloured fur and cascades of crystals. Musicians have turned hats into badges, flags and even sculptures. Hats are used to debunk or exaggerate, to dazzle or strike a pose, set a fashion, be eccentric, define, protect. They are the umbrellas of the soul.

Whatever the hat a musician chooses, and however they wear it, we expect magic to happen. Like a ringmaster raising his black topper, a musician in a hat compels us to stop everything and pay attention. We know a show is about to begin.

Lemmy of Motörhead PHIL KNOTT, 2000

Jamiroquai TIM O'SULLIVAN, 1993

Marc Bolan of T. Rex DAVID STEEN, 1973

MAURICE
CHEVALIER

Chevalier was a Parisian, and the very model of a charming dandy, with a ready wit, a smile on his face and bonhomie exuding from every pore. This natural showman's demeanour, combined with an elegant personality and a velvety voice marked the one-time cafe singer out for greatness.

The Parisian's voice was unmistakable, even when singing in impeccable English in American musicals such as *Gigi*. Equally unmistakable was the dapper angle of that straw boater. It was as though, rather than having to perform songs or recitations, he was about to set off for an afternoon jaunt on a sunny day. When discussing the object with a journalist he explained 'It's a man's hat. It's a gay hat. It's the hat to go with a tuxedo. From that moment I was never without a straw boater if I could help it, even when those hats went out of fashion.'

A straw boater was the faithful companion of many a performer, from the *cafés chantants* to the operetta and Italian vaudeville acts. It might not look like much, but it had proved itself an invaluable comic tool: with a straw boater in hand you just can't sing of desertion, tears, pain or broken hearts. Instead, you want to make others smile with a gesture, a joke and a tune to whistle on the way home.

Maurice Chevalier PHILIPPE HALSMAN, 1953

John Lennon of The Beatles DAVID HURN, 1964

Pete Doherty ALESSIO PIZZICANNELLA, 2006

Elton John TERRY O'NEILL, 1997

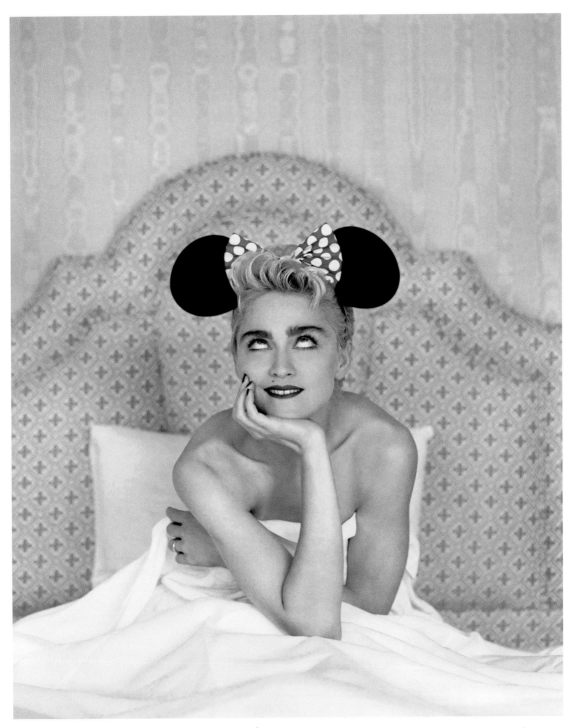

Madonna HERB RITTS, 1987

Little Steven EFREM RAIMONDI, 2000

Sun Ra GIUSEPPE PINO, 1976

Joni Mitchell GUIDO HARARI, 1998

Nina Hagen GUIDO HARARI, 1986

Michael Stipe of R.E.M. GUIDO HARARI, 1991

50 Cent CHESTER HIGGINS JR, 2003

Eminem UNIVERSAL STUDIOS, 2002

MILES DAVIS

To be a jazz icon like Miles Davis, you also have to be able to play like Miles Davis – that much is obvious. Sometimes, however, not even talent is enough: you also need the *physique du rôle*, the charisma. During Davis's early bebop years, his improvisations, lightning-fast changes and the clear, round sound of his trumpet all elicited powerful responses in audiences.

It was, however, Davis's tendency to judge quickly, and harshly. This irreverence, which was in contrast with the careful construction of his own image, meant he often attracted criticism and resentment. During a shoot with photographer Giuseppe Pino, Davis said that it was pointless to make Pino's assistant wipe the sweat from his skin; it would never become less black. This was typical of Davis, and Pino would get to know him well as he went on to take the trumpeter's portrait many times over the course of a career dedicated to photographing jazz.

Certain photographs of Davis became, for a while, like an emblem of personality. When the 17-year-old Giuseppe Pino saw the great Louis Armstrong in concert in the Teatro Lirico in Milan, he said: 'It's not enough to listen to music: you need to be able to watch it too. Louis was such a surprise: the man was definitely seen as well as felt. And I wanted to keep a souvenir of that, a photograph.' This sentiment could just have easily have been expressed about Davis's own performances: the face, the gaze, the way he stood on stage, all these elements were very much part of his music.

Unique in the history of jazz, Davis constantly innovated, sparking new music trends and influencing the development of generations of musicians. He was also an artist and an icon of pop culture and the entertainment industry. In this photograph Giuseppe Pino immortalized the spontaneity of Davis's gesture and his acute, ironic gaze against a background made up of infinite shades of blue. It is as if the lyrical, sensual, meditative atmosphere of *Kind of Blue* had become a photograph.

Miles Davis GIUSEPPE PINO, 1982

Count Basie EVERETT COLLECTION, 1972

Leonard Cohen MICHAEL DONALD, 2008

THE BLUES BROTHERS

This is a *Rolling Stone* cover from 1979. The Blues Brothers had been formed by comedy duo Dan Aykroyd and John Belushi only a year before. In 1980 their eponymously titled film would make them world famous, but for the moment there was only one album, *Briefcase Full of Blues*. Yet here they were on the cover of a prestigious music magazine.

Photographer Annie Leibovitz remembers: 'There's a case to be made that the simpler the idea the better. Putting blue paint on Dan Aykroyd and John Belushi, for instance. The first Blues Brothers album had gone double platinum, and they were taking themselves very seriously as musicians. I remember Belushi saying, "Did you hear Aykroyd on the harp? Better than Paul Butterfield!" Things were getting out of hand. I was thinking of them more as actors and comedians and I thought it would be funny to paint the Blues Brothers blue. I told Aykroyd and the writer, Tim White, what I had in mind. Neither of them thought that Belushi would go along with it. We took the photographs in a bungalow in West Hollywood that looked like a motel room. In most of the frames they're just horsing around on a bed. Jumping up and down with their sunglasses on. Their faces aren't painted. Then I asked the make-up artist to put the blue paint on and I managed to shoot eight or nine frames before Belushi stalked off. He didn't think it was funny at all. He didn't speak to me for six months.'

The Blues Brothers ANNIE LEIBOVITZ, 1979

Miles Davis DENNIS STOCK, 1958

WHEN THE NIGHT HAS COME

When the night has come / And the land is dark / And the moon is the only light we'll see / No I won't be afraid / Oh I won't be afraid / Just as long as you stand, stand by me Ben E. King

Thom Yorke, Radiohead
ALESSIO PIZZICANNELLA, 2003

T IS TRUE THAT many stories explaining the creation of the world begin simply with a sound or voice in the darkness, and this bond between music and the absence of light has endured. After all, it is in darkness that we experience many of the sensations that songs and music describe. Insomnia, fear of the unknown and the loneliness of the soul – often a simple lullaby, the most ancient and familiar of rhyming songs, can be a calming companion in the night. Darkness is also the time for sleeping, for dreaming, and, as Patti Smith sang 'the night belongs to lovers'.

There is something primordial about the experience of live music as the daylight fades. The stage lit against the darkness like a beacon and the music ringing out in the silence of the night are enough to send shivers down the spine. The dark backdrop intensifies what we hear and see.

It may sound like an overstatement, but the darkness is a blank sheet on which our dreams and desires can map themselves. It's also a time when music just sounds better. Music can also sustain us through the darkest of hours; as writer Jean Paul Richer once said, 'Music is moonlight in the gloomy night of life.'

Jazz has almost always been a celebration of the night, and ever since it emerged from its underground ragtime existence in bars and vaudeville shows, its language has evoked the darkness. Late at night in the clubs of New York's 52nd Street the rebellious architects of bebop – characters such as Charlie Parker and Dizzy Gillespie – would congregate together. After the shows they would play for themselves, revelling in the freedom the night offered. But the night did not belong to jazz alone: blues, soul and rock 'n' roll were all drawn to

Johnny Laws ACHIM MULTHAUPT, 2003

Backstage at a Wynton Marsalis concert
GUY LE QUERREC, 2004

Bruce Springsteen, Bono and Patti Smith, singing 'Because the Night'
KEVIN MAZUR, 2009

the shadows. Artists such as Tom Waits sung like they had been out all night, every night, searching for some kind of self-destructive redemption. Lou Reed, too, knew well what went on after dark. His lyrics are the story of New York city's wild side, a place of parties, drug deals and sadomasochism that only woke up once the sun had gone.

Modern music concerts, almost without exception, take place when it is dark, and this is not just because we only go out once the duties of the day are done. Concerts are held in the evening because the dusk and darkness enhance the mysteriousness that is still at the centre of music. Things may be clear in the day, but in the night ambiguity reigns and our sensitivity to light, sound and opportunity are all enhanced. Once the concert is over there is nothing more to do but go home and to dream.

Jim Morrison, The Doors ELLIOTT LANDY, 1968

Dexter Gordon, Freddie Hubbard, Ron Carter GUY LE QUERREC, 1985

Bill Evans GIUSEPPE PINO, 1967

Chet Baker GUY LE QUERREC, 1988

Frank Sinatra F. DRIGGS COLLECTION, 1954

Archie Shepp GUY LE QUERREC, 1996

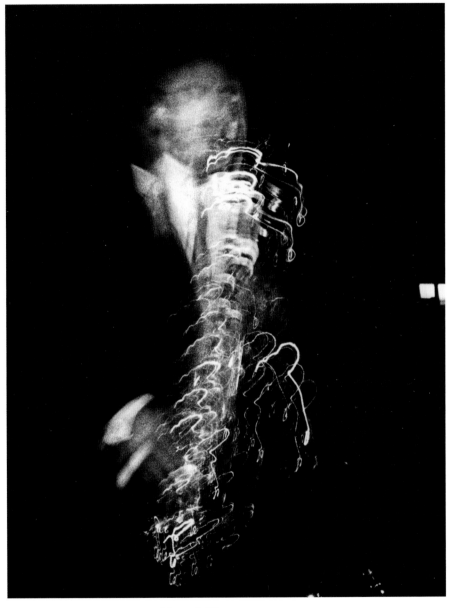

Johnny Griffin GIUSEPPE PINO, 1966

The French Quarter of New Orleans PAOLO PELLEGRIN, 2005

The Beatles PHILIP JONES GRIFFITHS, 1961

The shadow of Louis Sclavis at the Saint Louis International Jazz Festival in Senegal GUY LE QUERREC, 1993

Jimi Hendrix EVERETT COLLECTION, 1960S

Lou Reed and Laurie Anderson GUIDO HARARI, 2005

Bryan Ferry ANTON CORBIJN, 1992

Dave Gahan of Depeche Mode ANTON CORBIJN, 1992

Amy Winehouse MARCELLO BONFANTI, 2008

Diana Ross BRUCE DAVIDSON, 1965

SAMMY DAVIS JR

The 1950s in New York were a truly fabulous, glittering time. The city was in ferment, filled with artists and musicians who populated and enlivened its nights. The Copacabana was one of the most famous nightclubs of the period and Sammy Davis Jr often appeared on its stage. In 1959, after Davis's final show, Magnum photographer Burt Glinn took a portrait of this extraordinary African American singer–dancer–actor–comedian in the pale light of a New York dawn.

Madison Avenue, normally crowded with traffic, was virtually deserted at that time of day. Sammy Davis could stand in the middle of the street as if he were on stage, transforming the Avenue into his very own backdrop. Glinn's black and white photograph immortalized it all: the performer's irrepressible energy, the dreamlike silence of the sleeping city, the delicate tracks of snow on asphalt like the wooden planks of a vast stage.

New York was Sammy Davis Jr's city. He was born in Harlem and became part of the famous Rat Pack, sharing the stage with Frank Sinatra and Dean Martin in films such as *Ocean's Eleven*. Though this multi-talented figure was not always particularly popular with the black community, in his own way he played an important role in the struggle against racial segregation. Davis and the Rat Pack refused to perform or appear in places that discriminated against black people, often leading the nightclubs of Miami and the casinos of Las Vegas to change their policy. In his inimitably self-deprecating style, Davis announced 'Being a star has made it possible for me to get insulted in places where the average Negro could never hope to go and get insulted.' On that night in 1959, on that deserted street, with Glinn's perfect composition, New York truly belonged to him.

Sammy Davis Jr BURT GLINN, 1959

Louis Armstrong PHILIPPE HALSMAN, 1966

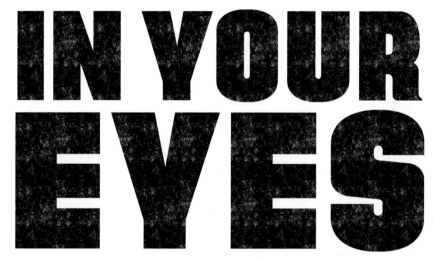

IN YOUR EYES

In your eyes the light the heat / In your eyes I am complete / In your eyes I see the doorway to a thousand churches / In your eyes the resolution of all the fruitless searches Peter Gabriel

YES OF ARTISTS can be the most dangerous and alluring eyes in the world, and a musician's eyes are no exception. Often, above all other features, the eyes epitomize the character and that shining star quality. Although, with the eyes of some dazzling supernovas of the music world, you wonder if there is a chance they might eventually collapse in on themselves, like black holes. Syd Barrett's eyes, for example. Even in photographs his eyes look out pin sharp, provoking a feeling of discomfort. They stare straight at you and through you, appearing to see things that the rest of us don't.

Then there are the eyes of a musician at work, seemingly indifferent, but really lost in a spiral of notes. At that moment a musician might seem to be aware of only themselves and the music, but then they suddenly look out and break the fourth wall with a gaze of incredible intensity, such as the one Jimi Hendrix gave the camera during his performance of 'The Star-Spangled Banner' at Woodstock. In that moment, it seemed as if time itself has stopped, and that Hendrix could see into the future.

There are also eyes that complete androgynous faces, such as those of Elvis Presley and Jim Morrison. Their eyes are part of what seem to be masks, appearances feminine enough to disturb all perceived certainties, with a softness of feature that evokes all the ambiguities of adolescence. These eyes were raised to the world framed by rebellious curls and smooth cheeks.

If we think of David Bowie's eyes (which, aptly, appear to be different colours) it seems almost too fitting – too perfectly matched to his unique stage act – to be an accident. The difference between his pupils is actually the result of a childhood accident, but the question remains: did he become the flamboyant Bowie we know because of his mismatching eyes?

It is clear that the music of our time is marked out by a series of faces, faces which, over time, have come to stand as symbols for the music they make. For many, that wide-eyed mien

Nina Simone
CAROL FRIEDMAN, 1995

Skin MARK C. O'FLAHERTY, 2003

Lou Reed GARRY GROSS, 1979

of Armstrong is jazz. Classic looks, styles and expressions are then constantly appropriated by new artists looking to glean the authority of a past master. Expressions recreated so many times that they obtain mythic status.

Once upon a time artists kept themselves aloof, and only photographers were allowed to approach them. Today, these faces and gazes are constantly under scrutiny and endlessly exposed. The same technology that allows photographs to be digitally improved for merchandise and magazines allows the internet generation to tamper with images at the expense of the musicians who, once captured in a photograph, cannot escape.

These photos have made us familiar with every detail of an artist's expression. We know how some singers tend to close their eyes when they sing, as if they feel the need to shut themselves off, searching within themselves for the sound. There are some eyes that can withstand the violence of the strong lighting, and then there are others, such as those of Annie Lennox and Sinéad O'Connor, that can hold an audience's undivided attention for entire music videos.

Leonard Cohen GUIDO HARARI, 1989

David Bowie CAROLYN DJANOGLY, 1999

Keith Richards of The Rolling Stones JANE BOWN, 1996

Chuck Berry H.D., 1970

Annie Lennox of Eurythmics ARISTA RECORDS, 2000

THE DOORS

The Doors brought out their self-titled debut album on 4 January 1967. Their music, born in Venice Beach, California, was a truly original mixture of psychedelica, rock, blues and theatre.

Jim Morrison (known as the 'Lizard King') had a baritone voice, was a hypnotic poet, had a talent for composing and was one of the most seductive personalities in the history of rock music. His dark and powerful features were softened by an unusual elegance, yet on stage he was a satyr in leather trousers. Jim drank, screamed and cried out, and his dancing roused his audiences as he strove to create a kind of bond with them. After arriving in Paris in 1971, just a few days before his death, Jim issued his last statement to the press: 'For me, it was never really an act, those so-called performances. It was a life-and-death thing; an attempt to communicate, to involve many people in a private world of thought.'

This statement perfectly describes the energy in 'Light My Fire', or the oedipal nightmare of 'The End', songs that are at first muted and suppressed, then explode. The Doors combined music with poetry, theatricality and drama, creating a visceral experience that involved all the senses. Jim Morrison, who died at the age of 27, was one of the best, and most enigmatic frontmen to have performed on stage.

Jim Morrison of The Doors KEYSTONE PICTURES USA, 1965

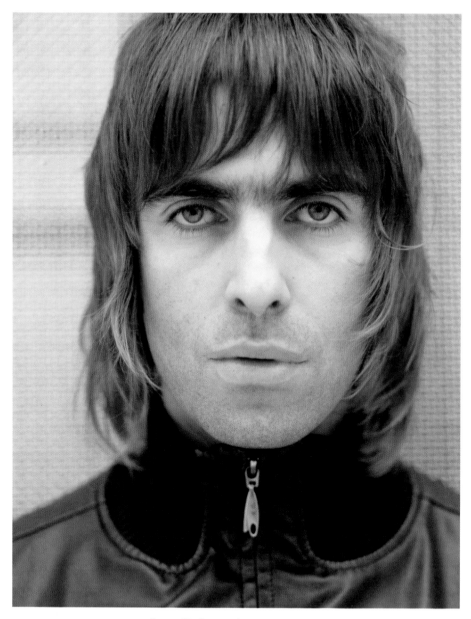

Liam Gallagher, Oasis PEBBLES CLINTON, 2000

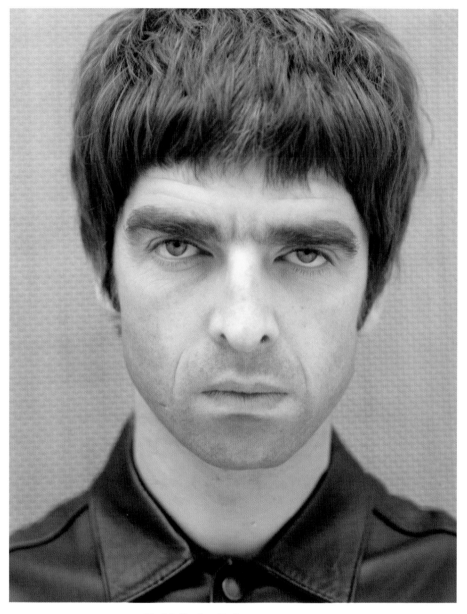

Noel Gallagher, Oasis PEBBLES CLINTON, 2000

Sinéad O'Connor GUIDO HARARI, 1988

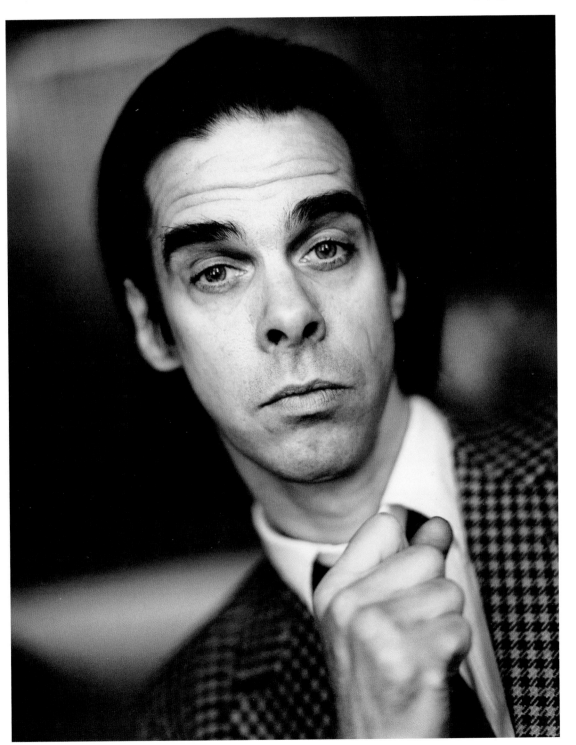

Nick Cave MORTEN LARSEN, 2001

Robbie Williams PHIL KNOTT, 2000

Björk KEVIN CUMMINS, 1990

Joan Baez YOUSUF KARSH, 1971

Jeff Buckley MICHEL LINSSEN, 2000

Iggy Pop NEIL COOPER, 1993

Marilyn Manson MICHAEL SPRINGER, 2000

Frank Zappa GIUSEPPE PINO, 1975

Kurt Cobain of Nirvana JULIAN BROAD, 1991

Brian Eno GIJSBERT HANEKROOT, 1974

Eddie 'Cleanhead' Vinson GIUSEPPE PINO, 1971

JOHN LENNON

Face set, he stares straight into the camera, the look in his eyes hovering somewhere between a frown and a sneer. It was 1964, and John Lennon was 24 years old, his difficult childhood and adolescence now behind him. By this age he was already (secretly) married with a son and, above all, was a key figure in the group that was changing the history of music.

For The Beatles, 1964 must have seemed like an endless year. They regularly topped the British pop charts, played concert after concert in front of delirious crowds and had launched their conquest of America with the single, 'I Want To Hold Your Hand'. After their enormously popular US television debut on the *Ed Sullivan Show*, the States fell at their feet. Part of the appeal was the 'smart young man' look that their manager, Brian Epstein, cultivated. Lennon, the most rebellious of the four, found it hard to accept, saying 'The Mop Top image was the kind of thing that happens when you're finally cornered in school, and you either had to just get smashed completely – or – I'm not going to get myself crucified, if I can help it, and so I've compromised. But I just want to see someone who hasn't and who's still alive!'

Along with the other three Beatles, John Lennon soon liberated himself from the threat of being stuck in the rut of bourgeois respectability: he grew his hair long, wore little round glasses, adopted a confrontational attitude and experimented with LSD. It is still a matter of debate as to who was the true genius of The Beatles; but it can safely be said that, of the Fab Four, Lennon had the most surreal talent for warped inventiveness. He was certainly the most provocative, causing outrage in 1966 by declaring to the *London Evening Standard*: 'We're more popular than Jesus now; I don't know which will go first – rock and roll or Christianity.'

It was also Lennon who, after meeting Yoko Ono during the middle of the 1960s, began to introduce the band to a more experimental musical language of love and peace. Yoko Ono also led Lennon towards a greater engagement with pacifism, and he became a champion of various protest movement. In 1980 he said to a journalist from *Rolling Stone*: 'What they [his fans] want is dead heroes, like Sid Vicious and James Dean. I'm not interested in being a dead f---ing hero.' Three days later he was killed by a delusional fan. The world mourned him and on the evening after his death Bruce Springsteen opened a concert by proclaiming: 'If it wasn't for John Lennon, we'd all be someplace very different tonight.'

John Lennon of The Beatles EVERETT COLLECTION, 1964

Chad Smith and John Frusciante, Red Hot Chili Peppers SARAH LEE, 1999

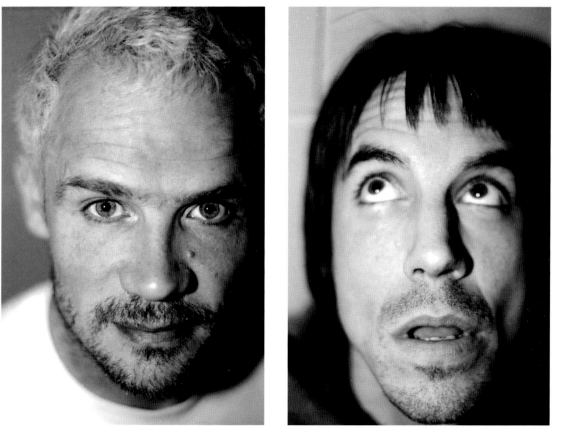

Flea and Anthony Kiedis, Red Hot Chili Peppers SARAH LEE, 1999

Jerry Garcia of the Grateful Dead BARON WOLMAN, 1969

Elvis Costello TERRY O'NEILL, 1989

Tom Waits GUIDO HARARI, 1999

Dave Stewart of Eurythmics LYNN GOLDSMITH, 1984

Cesaria Evora GUY LE QUERREC, 1995

LAURIE
ANDERSON

Laurie Anderson is a composer, writer, film-maker, photographer, ventriloquist, instrumentalist, electronic enchantress and performer. The polymath of the New York underground scene, she is cerebral and refined, provocative and ironic, as hypnotic as her gaze, and – as this photograph shows – relaxed in front of the camera.

The portrait was taken by Guido Harari, a photographer and music critic with whom both Anderson and her partner, Lou Reed, have developed a special friendship. Back in the 1970s, Harari embarked on a novel career in freelance photography, taking pictures only of those artists that he felt were in tune with his own sensibility and musical passions. Since then his photographs have been used on the covers of albums by Kate Bush, Paul McCartney, Bob Dylan and Frank Zappa. How could Harari fail to be fascinated by an artist as eclectic and original as Laurie Anderson?

Her songs are multimedia performances with a dreamlike atmosphere that slowly develops, eventually bringing together body and voice, music and story, singing and recitation. 'When I first made my CD ROM, I thought: "Here's a medium that includes images, sound and electronics and I can mix them." In fact, what was really interesting about it was that this kind of digital art making is very much the way my mind works, which is not in a narrative line but is about how things relate to each other....It's very circular and very much about points along the way. I just like the travel. If it is interesting enough, I don't care about getting there.'

Laurie Anderson GUIDO HARARI, 1990

Édith Piaf JEAN MARK LOUBAT, 1948

CAUGHT IN THE SPOT LIGHT

See the man with the stage fright / Just standin' up there to give it all his might / And he got caught in the spotlight / But when we get to the end / He wants to start all over again The Band

The Beatles at Shea Stadium in New York
BETTMANN, 1966

Beatles fans at a concert in Milan
GIORGIO LOTTI, 1965

NSIDE OR OUTSIDE, anywhere can be a stage. Throughout history, music has been heard in a whole host of locations: natural spaces, temporarily occupied by ancient rites or modern festivals; travelling stages set up in a new location every night by itinerant performers; in giant sports centres, adapted for the ritual of music; in bars, *boîtes*, exclusive clubs and, of course, theatres. Nobody who has ever appeared on stage ever forgets the feel of the wooden planks beneath their feet, the smells and the sights hidden in the wings, the sound of a restless, expectant crowd.

Over time, particular kinds of music have discovered their perfect stage, finding it perhaps in the remote countryside, or at the centre of a city, in ancient ruins, or in starkly modern surroundings. The stages used for rock music have become almost like dreamlands, arenas filled with pyrotechnics and extravagant props, a demonstration not only of rock's outlandish imagination, but also of the incredible funding behind music.

Pink Floyd's drummer, Nick Mason (who trained as an architect before the band took off) once suggested that music was the best area for an architect to work in. He must have had Pink Floyd's live shows in mind when he said it. During various performances the band have managed to turn the stage into a vast theatrical machine, variously equipped with a giant eye,

Iron Maiden MICK HUTSON, 2003

enormous robotic puppets, aircraft that flew over the audience, and even a mighty wall that grew to separate the musicians from the spectators. In 1989, Pink Floyd even went so far as to turn the city of Venice into a physical extension of the stage.

These experimental and avant-garde performances eventually even began to draw on everyday normality for their subjects and themes. During the golden age of their live performances (the *Zoo TV* and *PopMart* tours), U2 were able to simultaneously embrace the future of telecommunications technology, while pastiching the banality of television news and entertainment.

Throughout its history, rock has indulged itself with tricks of every kind, from Peter Gabriel's luminous robots to the epic lips of Rolling Stones shows. These bizarre sets show just how much lascivious bombast can be involved in celebrating rock; indeed some of the world's most astonishing spectacles have been staged in the name of music.

Frank Sinatra DENNIS STOCK, 1961

Nat King Cole PHIL STERN, C. 1940

Duke Ellington GIUSEPPE PINO, 1967

Juliette Gréco GAMMA, 1966

VENICE BEACH

For a long and unforgettable time music was the expression of freedom and unity for a whole generation. Rock was a language powerful enough to change the world – at least that's how it felt in California in 1968. Thousands of young people came together on Venice Beach to listen to music and invent their own American Dream, a dream that would be revolutionary on both personal and international scales.

Dennis Stock, a Magnum photographer, loved this wind of change and those who had gone in search of it: 'My subjects – the bikers, hippies, road people, artists – are simply people who have sought a less conforming way to explore this conforming life that we all lead. It was my fascination with their ability to survive as individuals that kept my camera busy.'

The air that ruffles the girl's hair carries something new. The movement of her arms and body, as she surrenders to the music and the sun of California, show her as carefree and contemporary in an emancipated age. She is like a vision rising above the crowded beach. Dennis Stock saw her and caught the perfect image, one which expresses the essence and atmosphere of a time and a place, and became one of the most famous photographs in American history.

Venice Beach Rock Festival DENNIS STOCK, 1968

Woodstock Festival

ELLIOTT LANDY, 1969

WOODSTOCK

The 17 August, 1969, was a Sunday like no other. It marked the end of the Woodstock Festival, an event remembered as the most famous concert in the history of music. Performances had started at 5 p.m. on Friday, with the opening day dedicated to folk music. Richie Havens and his Acoustic Guild appeared first on stage. He addressed the sea of young people: 'You know, we've finally made it. We did it this time. They'll never be able to hide us again.' The applause that followed filled the air with electricity.

Joan Baez was the headline act on that first day, and the five-month pregnant folk superstar appeared on stage at midnight. The protest music of folk was especially important in 1969; everyone was conscious of the violence in Vietnam, which seemed a lifetime away from this shared moment of belief and empathy. These were the years when it seemed certain that music was a language both eloquent and direct enough to change the world.

The Saturday was the triumph of rock and psychedelia. Acts including Santana, The Grateful Dead and Janis Joplin followed one another across the stage. At four in the morning The Who arrived and fired up the audience with a set that lasted for over two hours.

At around two in the afternoon on Sunday, Joe Cocker – then a virtually unknown Englishman – appeared on stage accompanied by the Grease Band. He opened the day's proceedings, astonishing everyone with a legendary cover of 'With a Little Help from My Friends' by The Beatles. On the meadow in front of him, about 500,000 people enjoyed another endless day of music. In fact, it still hadn't ended by Monday morning. At 3:30 a.m. the most eagerly awaited group of all, Crosby, Stills, Nash & Young, took to the stage. And still it did not end. As the sun rose, just before 9 a.m., Jimi Hendrix give a performance that would last more than two hours, the longest of his career. Among the pieces he played was his famous distorted version of the American national anthem, which emerged, howling from his guitar. Michael Lang, one of the organizers of the festival wrote: 'It was over. What had seemed an eternity now felt like the blink of an eye. Nothing would ever be the same again.'

Joe Cocker at Woodstock ELLIOTT LANDY, 1969

Anita Pallenberg and Marianne Faithfull at a Rolling Stones concert in Hyde Park BETTMANN, 1969

Jimi Hendrix JIM MARSHALL, 1974

THE BEATLES

It was a typically cold January morning in London, but by lunchtime the peace of the sombre, stuffy heart of the capital had been shattered by the sound of amplifiers. Music flooded through the streets and surrounding buildings, passers-by gazed upwards, searching for the source of the noise. People in nearby buildings, attracted by the music, looked out of their windows, while others, still wearing shirts and ties, climbed out onto office roofs. It was not a youthful or 'hip' part of town, but slowly a disbelieving crowd began to assemble. The Beatles' rooftop concert, the band's most memorable and punk-like gesture, was to be their last live performance.

It wasn't meant to be like that, though. The Beatles were putting on the live show for their documentary film *Let It Be*, and the performance was intended to demonstrate that the band wanted to go back to performing live after years of recording in studios without touring. They had had various ideas for the gig: an anonymous concert in a little German club, or perhaps a live show in the ruins of a Roman amphitheatre in the desert. Time was short, however, and the final decision was made for the band to play on the roof of Apple Corps Ltd (the multimedia corporation founded by the Fab Four) on Savile Row.

The legendary gig started with 'Get Back', and continued with 'Don't Let Me Down', a heartfelt 'I've Got a Feeling', 'One After 909' and 'Dig a Pony', as well as alternative versions of the first three pieces. Forty-two minutes of music turned the workaday routine of those passing below clutching bowler hats and briefcases upside down. Then the police arrived to restore calm; however, as it was pop royalty The Beatles who were disturbing the public order, there was no question of just switching off the amplifiers. The officers let Paul McCartney finish singing 'Get Back' (while he improvised, among other things, a verse that teased them a little) and then it was time to go. And so, on 30 January 1969, the Fab Four's final performance ended, with John Lennon waving and saying as he left: 'I hope we passed the audition.'

The Beatles on the roof of Apple Corps Ltd RBO, 1969

Abba GEORGE ROSE, 1981

A Sex Pistols concert DENNIS MORRIS, 1977

The Bangles EVERETT COLLECTION, 1984

Crosby, Stills, Nash & Young
EVERETT COLLECTION, 1970S

SIMON
& GARFUNKEL

Central Park, on a warm evening in the middle of September, was the perfect setting for an event that felt at once both nostalgic and epic. It had been suggested to Paul Simon that he should play a concert in New York's Central Park, and so, in September 1981, the incredible Simon and Garfunkel reunion finally happened. After eleven years of separate solo careers, the two old friends found themselves on stage in front of a sea of 500,000 people, surrounded by the scenic backdrop of the city's skyscrapers.

The sound of the crowd must have been deafening and, for the first few minutes, Art Garfunkel kept rubbing his hands together in a way that hinted at a deep, and perhaps unexpected, wave of emotion. Then Paul Simon struck up 'Mrs. Robinson' and it seemed as if all of New York was there singing along with their two calm voices, melodies that brought back the glory years of the 1960s.

This performance was recorded and released as *The Concert in Central Park*, one of the duo's best known albums. In his *Rolling Stone* review, Stephen Holden wrote: 'One reason the Central Park concert was so memorable is Simon and Garfunkel's special relationship to New York City. Unlike many of the Gotham-bred pop stars of their generation who made it big, these nice Jewish boys from Queens didn't run off to Malibu to live happily ever after, once they were millionaires. They stayed around the city, continuing to assimilate its cultural resources, recycle them and give them back. The sense of a lifelong romance with New York permeates the record.'

Simon and Garfunkel in Central Park EBET ROBERTS, 1981

The Rolling Stones' Urban Jungle Europe Tour GRAHAM WILTSHIRE, 1990

Roger Waters used to tell anyone who asked that he would never again perform *The Wall*, his epic rock opera about dehumanization and alienation. But in July 1989, when a journalist asked him the same question for the umpteenth time, he said: 'OK, we could do it on stage, but only if the Berlin Wall falls. In that case it would be an act of celebration of the liberation of the human spirit.' Four months later the Berlin Wall did indeed come down, and on 21 July 1990 Waters staged *The Wall* once again.

In the no-man's-land of Potsdamer Platz, which had been trapped between East and West Berlin for nearly three decades, Roger Waters mounted one of the largest, most ambitious, most spectacular live events ever created. After having been a barren space for so many years, Potsdamer Platz became the centre of the world for a day. More than 300,000 people were lucky enough to be there in front of the stage, while something like 100 million people watched it live on television. A gigantic stage 'wall', 170 metres long, confronted the audience, and from an enormous crane were suspended sophisticated and surreal humanoid puppets. One of the figures, 'the Teacher', had a colossal drooping head that loomed menacingly over the stage, peering at the audience with searchlight eyes.

Roger Waters and a succession of other artists gave both form and voice to the characters from his extremely vivid imagination. In a breathtaking crescendo at the end of 'The Trial' the stage 'wall' was knocked down, echoing world events. The concert ended with a firework display, while on stage Waters, his guest artists and the Berlin Radio Symphony Orchestra sang 'The Tide Is Turning'. The tide really was turning. In this place, which had come to symbolize division and oppression, rock music had once again raised the cry for rebellion and freedom.

Following pages **Pink Floyd in Venice** LUCIANO VITI, 1988

The Wall Concert, Berlin ROB WERHORST, 1990

Genesis MATTIA ZOPPELLARO, 2007

Depeche Mode LOUISE STICKLAND, 2009

ELTON JOHN

'I remember hearing Elton John's 'Your Song' in America', said John Lennon, 'I remember thinking, great, that's the first new thing that's happened since we happened. It was a step forward. There was something about his vocals that was an improvement on all of the English vocals until then.'

'Your Song', released in 1970, was destined to become both an evergreen classic and the soundtrack to countless love stories. With the assistance of Bernie Taupin (who co-wrote the lyrics to his songs) Elton John dominated the American and British charts throughout the 1970s. His concerts around the world would often sell out completely, and among his fans there were scenes of hysteria and delirium – even in Leningrad when he played there in 1979.

His live performances from these years are his strongest work. In a period when the guitar usually reigned supreme, Elton John brought the piano back to the centre of the stage, making it a key rock instrument once more. Following the example of the masterful Jerry Lee Lewis, Elton's piano performances were frenetic and theatrical. He astonished the public with acrobatic keyboard handstands that showed off his heels and platform soles.

Elton's look was a vital element of his stage presence; it wasn't just the bizarre shapes of his glasses that defined his style, but also the costumes and elaborate fancy dress that he wore. The outfits toyed with ideas of kitsch and ambiguous sexuality. The other gods of glam rock, including rival David Bowie, did the same. Critics turned up their noses, preferring to see a sober and composed English pianist, but Elton John took a different view: 'At the start, the critics loved my music, but when I started to dress up, they all said it was pointless. They'd have preferred me to go on stage in jeans and a T-shirt. But that wouldn't have been me.' The public loved what he did and carried on filling the stadiums.

Following pages **Bono, Zooropa tour** ROGER HUTCHINGS, 1993

Elton John TERRY O'NEILL, 1970S

PETER GABRIEL

He stands on the edge of the stage, his back to the crowd. A cry goes up and Peter Gabriel closes his eyes, allowing himself to fall into the outstretched arms of the yelling crowd. His body is carried away by a current of hands moving together. Stage diving is symbolic of a deeply 'rock' attitude. It is all about the adrenalin that comes with knowing that there is no safety net, abandoning the body to the unexpected and losing control.

Back in the 1980s it was Peter Gabriel (the lead singer of Genesis) and Iggy Pop who invented and popularized this extreme gesture of merging and sharing with the audience. Throughout Genesis's heyday, the visual impact of live performances was fundamental for the band: Peter Gabriel dominated the stage, enthralling audiences with his theatrical presence, bizarre costumes and make-up.

It was during a performance of 'The Knife' in 1971 that Gabriel – swept up by the rhythm of the song – first threw himself into the crowd, in doing so breaking his leg. He was carried back to the stage and went on to finish the concert.

Peter Gabriel in Oakland NEAL PRESTON, 1988

Peter Gabriel in Abidjan NEAL PRESTON, 1988

Peter Gabriel in Los Angeles NEAL PRESTON, 1988

MADONNA

Andreas Gursky's image is a particular point of view, both a vision and a reflection. On 13 September 2001, Madonna was playing the Staples Center in Los Angeles on her *Drowned World Tour*. The concert, originally planned for 11 September, had been postponed because of the terrorist attack on the World Trade Center. Emotions were running high.

A highly regarded German artist, Gursky took up a position to the right of the stage and photographed the event from above. From this elevated vantage point he could let his camera wander over the vast crowd, so large that it monopolized the whole scene.

The final image became a work of abstraction. During processing, Gursky fused multiple photographs of the same concert into a single image, entitling the photo *Madonna I* and printing it in an extra-large format: 2 by 2.75 metres. The effect is spectacular. The artist did not simply recreate the space of this event, but instead created an image filled with distorted perspectives and proportions. The result is a dramatic composition, in which the focus is not only on the star but also on the blurred sea of the audience that surrounds her.

Madonna is a tiny figure on stage to the left of the image, wearing the American flag in solidarity. The lights illuminate her as she faces the enthusiastic crowd. But a sense of menace seems to have entered the scene: the distorted proportions give the image a disquieting feeling of uncertainty and unease, which subtly fractures the glossy surface of a huge pop concert that had been planned and prepared down to the very last detail.

Madonna in Los Angeles ANDREAS GURSKY, 2001

Christina Aguilera UPI, 2010

Mick Jagger, The Rolling Stones RICHARD YOUNG, 1969

Following pages **Rihanna** VEGAS 5, 2010

Freddie Mercury, Queen GEORGE ROSE, 1978

David Bowie ANTON CORBIJN, 1980

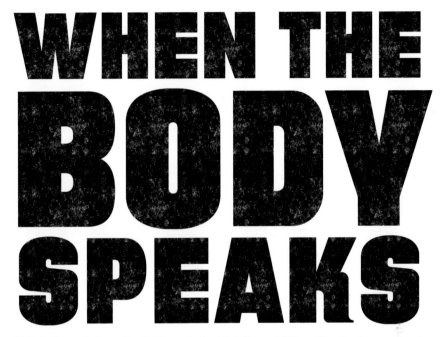

WHEN THE BODY SPEAKS

What the spirit seeks / The mind will follow / When the body speaks / All else is hollow Depeche Mode

Madonna
NEAL PRESTON, 1990

HE BODY IS the temple of
the human spirit, the home
of our every emotion and
the origin of every possible
rhythm. It is where the breath
of our voices resides and it is the means of
control for the blowing, bowing, strumming
and striking that turn instruments from
inanimate objects into living things.

'When the body speaks', sang Dave Gahan
of Depeche Mode, 'all else is hollow'. He delivered this line with bare torso and outstretched
arms, as if surrendering himself – flesh, bones and tattoo-etched skin – to the audience. Taken
out of context this scene could seem more like an image of human sacrifice during ancient
rites, but luckily the world no longer requires such offerings. The ancient attitude has,
however, transferred itself into music, and some artists will go to any length to draw attention
to their bodies. They sweat, stretch out, kneel, convulse, spasm and some have even crucified
themselves – many doing so in an effort to impress on the audience the importance of the body.

On stage, stars have dressed and moved to give themselves fantastical bodies, dismantled
bodies and even the bodies of robots and animals. Artists such as David Bowie and Sting have
at times focused on their appearance to an almost narcissistic degree, turning self-imaging
into a kind of art. Yet both classically beautiful bodies making supremely elegant movements,
or unique bodies in unnatural contortions can be equally, and compellingly, vivid.

Of all the ways the body can be used to express, dance has to be the most important. The
body's instinctive reaction to rhythm is to start moving, keeping time and marking out the

Michael Jackson
JACKY NAEGELEN, 1992

John Lennon and Yoko Ono
BLANK ARCHIVES, 1968

Eminem JASON BELL, 1999

beat – together the energy of the music meets the energy of the body in a duet. One could write whole novels about rhythm's cultural impact, and its differences. The rhythm of the Western world has grown in time signatures and meters, but rhythm elsewhere was passed on orally. When slaves were deported from Africa, they took with them their own songs and beats that were transformed and kept alive in those new islands and continents. Eventually their rhythms emerged in the West in the form of jazz, rhythm and blues, calypso, reggae and rock.

Of all these differing styles, it is perhaps rock music that most frantically affects the body, whipping listeners into a frenzy and even reaching the social and political contradictions at the heart of the West. It was certainly one of the most powerful movements in the twentieth century, causing us to dance, showing that we believe in the song enough to get up and move – exactly what Bob Marley meant when he sang: 'get up, stand up, stand up for your rights'. You can stand up for your rights by dancing, and getting others to dance. It's impossible to forget that – whatever lifestyle choices we make – if we choose to rebel, we need our bodies.

ELVIS

When Elvis appeared on stage in America in the middle of the 1950s, his raw, almost unconscious sensuality and swaying hips outraged the puritanical attitudes of many Americans. It had all begun in 1954, when he cut 'That's All Right (Mama)'; not only was it Elvis's first disc, but *Rolling Stone* later described it as the first true rock 'n' roll record in the history of music.

It was immediately obvious that Elvis wasn't just another teenage idol modelled on Frank Sinatra. His music was a shook-up mix of country, blues, pop and devastating stage presence. Moreover, it was a symptom of the wider, ongoing cultural revolution. The censors soon went to work on the singer, and in 1957 they insisted that 'Elvis the Pelvis' only be shown from the waist up when he appeared on television. But they were too late: Elvis was already the King, simultaneously embodying both the sins and virtues of America.

'He was as big as the whole country itself, as big as the whole dream', said Bruce Springsteen after Elvis died. 'He just embodied the essence of it and he was in mortal combat with the thing. Nothing will ever take the place of that guy....There have been a lot of tough guys. There have been pretenders. And there have been contenders. But there is only one king.'

Elvis Presley M.G.M., 1957

Yves Montand HERVÉ GLOAGUEN, c. 1960

JANIS JOPLIN

Janis was still singing with Big Brother and the Holding Company when she came to Bob Seidemann's studio for a photo session. The photographer's idea was to portray her nude from the waist up, with her wearing an open robe and a string of pearls. He shot a few rolls of black and white film and thought that the session was over. But then, remembers Seidemann, Janis took off all her clothes and asked him to photograph her nude. This photo, simultaneously so intimate and impudent, was published by *Rolling Stone* after Janis's death in 1970.

Produced during the Summer of Love, Joplin's robed portrait became a famous poster and sold more than 150,000 copies: an unprecedented number. Janis was the first female rock star, and she had more than demonstrated that a woman's voice could embody rock 'n' roll. Her performances were passionate, emotional and sensual; her presence electric and uninhibited; her style magnetic – it all combined to make her a symbol of the musical and social revolution of the 1960s. Janis was enthusiastic about these pictures and about the success of her poster; in a letter to her family, she wrote: 'Guess what, I might be the first Hippie pin-up girl.'

Janis Joplin BOB SEIDEMANN, 1967

Ozzy Osbourne TERRY SMITH, 1986

Sid Vicious, Sex Pistols BOB GRUEN, 1977

Marilyn Manson ALBERT WATSON, 1996

Tom Waits
GUIDO HARARI, 1992

PATTI SMITH

She is the poetess of rock, a skinny shamaness with fever in her voice and a visionary talent for blending words and music. He was one of America's most provocative and sophisticated photographers, who could transform pornographic images into high art. Their relationship was an artistic and soulful symbiosis.

Robert Mapplethorpe and Patti Smith met in the fervent atmosphere of late 1960s New York. They were both in their twenties and soon became friends and lovers, companions in their exploration of art and life itself. It was because: 'Nobody sees as we do, Patti', as Mapplethorpe was fond of saying to her, that they became and remained kindred spirits.

Patti Smith was Mapplethorpe's first model when he took up photography. His soft black and white images caught the wild expressions and intensity that Patti could conjure up with just a movement of her hand. Their sibling-like relationship, which bound the pair so closely together, allowed them to make great progress in their artistic development: Robert's work appeared in galleries and exhibitions, while Patti performed in New York's underground clubs.

Naturally (as her first and most passionate fan) it was Mapplethorpe who shot the intense black and white portrait of Patti that was used on the cover of her first album, *Horses*. In her memoir, *Just Kids*, Patti Smith remembered: 'One late afternoon, we were walking down Eighth Street when we heard 'Because the Night' blasting from one storefront after another. It was my collaboration with Bruce Springsteen, the single from the album *Easter*. Robert was our first listener, after we had recorded the song. I had a reason for that. It was what he always wanted for me. In the summer of 1978 it rose to number 13 on the Top 40 chart, fulfilling Robert's dream that I would one day have a hit record.' She was no longer just a cult figure, she was now definitively a rock star, and this was to a great extent due to the creative force of her friendship with Robert Mapplethorpe, who had changed her life. 'Robert and I had explored the frontier of our work and created space for each other. When I walked on the stages of the world without him I would close my eyes and picture him taking off his leather jacket, entering with me the infinite land of a thousand dances.'

Patti Smith ROBERT MAPPLETHORPE, 1978

Sting BRIAN ARIS, 1996

JOHN LENNON

& YOKO ONO

It would have been a memorable cover, but history intervened and made it legendary. The first 1981 issue of *Rolling Stone* was going to carry new photos of John Lennon and Yoko Ono, and publication was due to coincide with the release of their new album, *Double Fantasy*. On 8 December 1980 the magazine's best photographer, Annie Leibovitz, was welcomed by the couple like an old friend. She had, ten years earlier, already taken a striking portrait of John Lennon looking straight into the camera. The photograph had been taken as a test while measuring the light levels, but it had such a sincere intimacy that it ended up on the cover. This time, Annie intended to photograph the couple nude. John was delighted with the idea and quickly got undressed. Yoko was much less happy and so she decided, in consultation with Annie, that she would remain fully clothed. A nude John Lennon then wrapped himself around his wife, unafraid of showing his devotion or his physical fragility. Annie photographed them from above to create an extremely powerful image. They chose the cover picture together from a selection of Polaroid test photos.

That same night, just a few hours later, John Lennon was assassinated by a fan outside his apartment. The image of his nude figure, tenderly embracing Yoko Ono, was his last portrait. The photo appeared on the cover of *Rolling Stone* without a title or text, the first time this had happened in the magazine's history. There was no need to add anything else. The founder, Jann Wenner, wrote: 'Without any doubt, hands down, the greatest cover we've ever done.'

John Lennon and Yoko Ono ANNIE LEIBOVITZ, 1981

Beth Ditto of The Gossip MARY MCCARTNEY, 2007

Madonna MIRAMAX, 1991

Bono, U2 JIRI REZAC, 1993

Tina Turner MICHEL EINSSEN, 1990

KURT COBAIN

Rock music in the 1960s and 70s used and portrayed the body as a site and force for liberation. Sex, drugs and breaking the rules were not just ways of protesting, but ways of being and feeling free. By the end of the 1970s, however, the body had come to represent anger, hate and screaming protest. It neither recognized nor wanted revolutions; it was resigned, hopeless and no longer expected anything. Society had become loathsome and so had existence, and the only 'honesty' that remained, in terms of reaction to the experiences of life, was auto-destruction. Think of the wounds on Sid Vicious's body in 1977 and the scratches on Cobain's back more than ten years later; self-abuse was like a drug, a desperate attempt to relieve the suffering. Anger previously directed towards the world had now turned in upon itself, and so wounds and scars became a form of language that allowed one to communicate with other members of the same desperate tribe. The injuries also seemed to have a savage beauty that could be shown off, and it was left to the body to carry the imprint of nihilistic revolt. Cobain wrote in his diary: 'Please lord, f--k hit records, just let me have my very own unexplainable rare stomach disease named after me. And the title of our next double album, *Cobain's Disease*.'

Kurt Cobain of Nirvana ANTON CORBIJN, 1993

Iggy Pop GUIDO HARARI, 1979

Flea, Red Hot Chili Peppers GUIDO HARARI, 1995

Prince NEAL PRESTON, 1992

Lady Gaga MARCO GROB, 2010

Fabrizio De André GUIDO HARARI, 1979

WITH A BACKSTAGE PASS

And there were wackoes and weirdoes and dingbats and dodoes / And athletes and movie stars and David Alan Coe / There was leather and lace and every minority race / With a backstage pass to the Willie Nelson Show

Johnny Cash

**Nancy and
Sid Vicious**
DENNIS MORRIS, 1977

OME DRESSING ROOMS look like real rooms. And some certainly don't. Mick
Jagger's would have a throne-like armchair placed in the centre, from which
he would direct the dancing. Terence Trent D'Arby wanted his to be in semi-
darkness with one hundred lit candles on coloured cloths. Annie Lennox
preferred hers to have vintage-style rooms with mirrors surrounded by
white lightbulbs. Courtney Love would treat hers like a room in her own home: her clothes
scattered around, large sofas and a potable *gohonzon* so that she could perform the *gongyo*
(a Buddhist mantra).

Being backstage with Italian singer-songwriter Francesco Guccini is almost like attending
a restaurant, with gifts of tasty salamis and wines brought by his faithful friends littering
the tables. Others artists are more demanding and eccentric, expecting flowers, towels of
only one colour, certain vintages of wines, pinball machines or even a ping-pong table. Every
extravagance is allowed in the music world, and often the contracts specifying backstage
demands can run to hundreds of pages.

When large groups are on tour the backstage area becomes a hive of activity, swarming
with technicians, stagehands and press agents, however the star's accommodation is always
well protected and virtually inaccessible. From a certain point of view, backstage is a fabulous,
unknown place, where all fans would like to poke their noses, if only they had that backstage

Backstreet Boys ENRICO BOSSAN, 1997

Ringo Starr of The Beatles
PHILIP JONES GRIFFITHS, 1963

Barney Wilen
GUY LE QUERREC, 1995

pass allowing 'Access all Areas'. For those who don't, the imagination paints a place of fantasies and potential encounters.

The worst and most wild backstage behaviour in history has been mythologized in a vast number of memoirs, articles and rumours that seem to paint a picture of rock as a lustful Babylon. These stories are certainly not suitable for children, and – as are they often utterly unverified – perhaps they are hardly edifying for adults either. And excess is not always the case, of course. U2 are famous for their unsullied and ethically proper backstage arrangements. Should one wander into Led Zeppelin's territory, however, then that was indeed a cause for fear. They knew how to enjoy themselves in their glory days, and paid no heed to expense or limit: Led Zep were known as notorious libertines, who could transform the backstage area into a battlefield. Wrecking hotel rooms was also a favourite pastime for bands, and perhaps most famous of all was Keith Moon, who liked to play with dynamite.

The taste for excess has not disappeared entirely from music, and anyone taking a curious peek into Metallica's dressing rooms could be forgiven for doubting that music has cleaned up its act. But it is also true that backstage is the place where unique encounters occur; music is celebrated; musicians talk, share their feelings and celebrate the privilege of being in this artistic oasis. While it offers opportunities for all kinds of misbehaviour, it can also be a quiet and protected environment. And as any fan will tell you, the music is what really matters.

Billie Holiday PHIL STERN, 1955

MILES DAVIS

In May 1949 The International Festival of Jazz in the Salle Pleyel, Paris, brought together some of the biggest names in jazz: Charlie Parker, Sidney Bechet and Claude Luter all attended, along with pianist Tadd Dameron and Miles Davis. Davis, 23 at the time, cut a strangely beautiful and elegant figure; he had already played with the jazz greats and was well on his way to becoming one of the most influential and original musicians of the twentieth century.

Davis discovered Paris that May, and it was the start of an intense, long-term love affair – and not only with the city itself. 'This was my first trip out of the country and it changed the way I looked at things forever', wrote Davis in his autobiography. 'I loved being in Paris and loved the way I was treated….That was where I met Jean-Paul Sartre and Pablo Picasso and Juliette Gréco. I have never felt like that in my life since.' The young American trumpeter felt a new sense of freedom during this period and fell deeply in love. 'Music had been my total life until I met Juliette Gréco and she taught me what it was to love someone other than music. Juliette was probably the first woman that I loved as an equal human being. She was a beautiful person. We had to communicate with each other through expressions and body language. She didn't speak English and I didn't speak French. We talked through our eyes, fingers, stuff like that. When you communicate like that, you know the person is not bullshitting. You have to go on feelings.' Juliette was standing offstage in the wings when she saw him for the first time: 'I caught a glimpse of Miles, in profile: a real Giacometti, with a face of great beauty….There was such an unusual harmony between the man, the instrument and the sound – it was pretty shattering.' Their story became a legend because the relationship contained an element of the impossible: Davis had to go back to New York and a couple such as Davis and Gréco would be simply unacceptable in 1950s America. This was the start of a difficult personal period for Davis.

He found the disparity between the respect given to jazz musicians in France and the relative lack of interest he encountered in the US deeply depressing. In later years Miles Davis noted his return to the States and his separation from Gréco as the main causes of his drug dependency.

Miles Davis and Juliette Gréco ANDRE SAS, 1958

Elvis Presley BOB CAMPBELL, 1956

Following pages **Ian Curtis of Joy Division** KEVIN CUMMINS, 1979

Jimi Hendrix HENRY DILTZ, 1967

Enrico Rava and Mark Helias GUY LE QUERREC, 2001

Ed Sanders and Janis Joplin ELLIOTT LANDY, 1968

Ed Sanders and Janis Joplin ELLIOTT LANDY, 1968

Following pages **Blur** PAUL POSTLE, 1995

U2

PARAMOUNT
PICTURES, 1988

Vasco Rossi EFREM RAIMONDI, 2002

Tokio Hotel BAATZ, 2006

ALICE COOPER

'Without *Barbarella* there would be no Alice Cooper. When I saw Anita Pallenberg playing the Great Tyrant in that movie in 1968, wearing long black leather gloves with switchblades coming out of them, I thought, "That's what Alice should look like."'

Vincent Damon Furnier was originally the vocalist of Alice Cooper, inheriting the name as a solo artist when the band split up. He is now considered the godfather of the shock rock phenomenon, and among his godchildren are KISS, Ozzy Osbourne and Marilyn Manson.

Alice Cooper had begun by taking a hard look at the whole rock scene at the end of the 1960s: 'Why do we always have rock heroes? Why not a rock villain? I was more than happy to be rock's Darth Vader. I was more than happy to be Captain Hook', he said in an interview. A strange outfit, make-up, scandalous behaviour and highly theatrical performances filled with the paraphernalia of horror movies were all vital ingredients of his character. He sang 'No More Mr. Nice Guy' and used dark eyeliner to give his expression a demonic appearance. Alice Cooper's stage act involved guillotines, electric chairs, boa constrictors and fake blood. No one had done anything quite like it before. Excess was the rule, but a satirical vein of surrealism ran through it all, winning him many fans. Among his admirers was Salvador Dalí, who was so impressed that made a holographic portrait of Alice Cooper in full costume.

The contrast with the hippie bands of the early 1970s was striking, noted Alice Cooper: 'We were into fun, sex, death and money when everybody was into peace and love. We wanted to see what was next. It turned out we were next, and we drove a stake through the heart of the Love Generation.'

Who was really behind that demonic visage? 'Even my kids' says Furnier 'when Alice was on TV on *The Muppet Show*, said, "Look, there's Alice Cooper." They'd never say, "Look, there's Dad." They know that I just play Alice.'

Following pages **Édith Piaf** NICOLAS TIKHOMIROFF, 1961

Alice Cooper TERRY O'NEILL, 1973

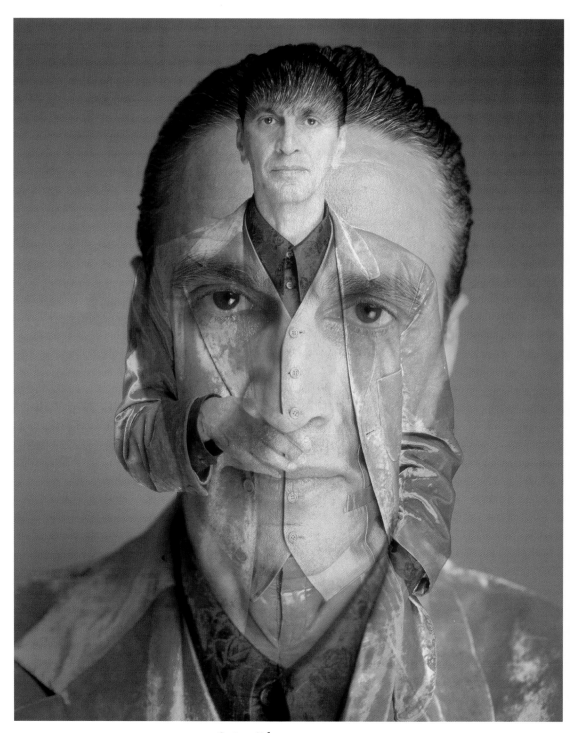

Caetano Veloso GUIDO HARARI, 1996

TAKE OFF THE MASK

I walk around, I'm suffering in my doom / When I come to you / You're sitting in your room / You sit around in the strangest place / So take off the mask / So I can see your face **Michael Jackson**

Eminem ROTA, 2001

HE MASK CONCEALS, or does it reveal? Music plays this game of pretence and exposure with consummate ease, moving endlessly between reality and representation to great effect. It removes the mask, and then replaces it, over and over again.

Carmen Miranda's towering fruit hats filled the screen; Sun Ra's space-age cloaks were like dancing celebrations of the cosmos; Liza Minnelli had her mask so indelibly imprinted on her face that that she could never remove it. In music it seems that the masks we place over our own faces, often merge with them in the end.

The sudden appearance of masks in rock music is usually ascribed to the genius of David Bowie who, from the very start of his career, approached the rock universe as a stage on which the right mask had always to be worn.

And what came before Bowie? There were attempts and flashes of inspiration, but nobody before him had created such a systematic and self-conscious body of work. The Beatles did wear walrus masks on one particular occasion, but their most brilliant use of costume was when they became Sgt. Pepper's Lonely Hearts Club Band. For the album The Beatles created their own doubles, a band that (freed from the pressures of being The Beatles and touring) could experiment with songs as full of kaleidoscopic effects and disguises as the performers.

On the whole, however, the golden age of music was in love with a quite different concept: the face, which was true, unequivocal and represented absolute sincerity. Bob Dylan and

Slipknot MIKE PERSSON, 2001

Michael Jackson THEODORE WOOD, 1996

Daft Punk
NICK WILSON, 2007

Jim Morrison sang about their own histories and lives, often without a filter of any kind. John Lennon refused to employ any artificial illusions to separate his art and life; rather he preferred that they overlapped and merged into one seamless whole. No one doubted that what Jimi Hendrix and Janis Joplin were presenting was indeed their own lives.

If an artist wasn't believable, he or she didn't stand a chance. So when the mask arrived it had a peculiar effect.

Alice Cooper didn't just throw on a mask, but developed a whole fearsome Grand Guignol style. Bowie liked to erase any trace of his true self. At this point it seemed that there were virtually no precedents. And then along came a group called The Residents. They didn't just wear masks, they used them as substitutes for their real faces, which they never reveal, attempting to keep their real identity a secret.

From Bono's little red horns to Bjork's rhinestone tears, masks in music have always been a way of drawing attention to oneself, and hiding at the same time. When you least expect it, a artist will appear wearing a mask: it's just their way of saying 'Boo!' from the masked ball that is the world of music.

JOHN LENNON

Artifice is an essential element of performance: disguises allow the artist and the audience to make contact. Masks and make-up can conceal, confuse, theatricalize or transform characters. Success often produces a similar effect, and celebrities can change according to the demands of their fame. The artist can never 'just' be themselves, as they are simultaneously the living proof of their own backstory, and seen as a commentary on their own art.

John Lennon had a great sense of humour, as Bob Whitaker (the photographer who took the many of the most famous and controversial pictures of The Beatles) remembers. The two became friends in 1964, and Whitaker accompanied the group on their second tour of America. In 1965, they created this delicate (and ironic) image together. The Fab Four had already achieved renown, with one tour following another in quick succession – the whole world was crazy about them.

John Lennon often reflected on the meaning of being a rock star, and on the restrictions the image imposed on him. 'I'm not a tough guy. I've always had to have a façade of being tough to protect myself from other people's neuroses. But really, I'm a very sensitive, weak guy.' Fame was exciting, but could sometimes feel as hectic as a three-ring circus. All Lennon could do was put on his best disguise. 'I would find myself seeing hallucinatory images of my face changing and becoming cosmic and complete. It caused me to always be a rebel. This thing gave me a chip on the shoulder; but, on the other hand, I wanted to be loved and accepted. Part of me would like to be accepted by all facets of society and not be this loudmouthed lunatic musician. But I cannot be what I am not.'

John Lennon of The Beatles BOB WHITAKER, 1965

Mick Jagger of The Rolling Stones ALBERT WATSON, 1992

MICK JAGGER

There are few figures so naturally provocative and libidinous as Mick Jagger; along with The Rolling Stones he managed to both incarnate and articulate the animalistic nature of rock music.

With a face that was old before its time, combined with the pouting lips and supple body of a teenager, Jagger has always been a fascinating sex symbol. There is little doubt that his face is one of the most sensual in rock – it is certainly one of the most photographed. It was his mouth that became the logo of The Rolling Stones, a symbol that still powerfully evokes the attraction and transgression of the dark side of music (an association that their own lyrics have encouraged). On stage, Jagger prowls like an animal. He has the look of a born seducer, someone who has enjoyed every excess – in short he has the look of the archetypal rock star.

For a photographer, going on tour with The Rolling Stones would be a challenge not only to get the right photographs, but also to survive in the jungle of psychedelic excess where the band lived. One explorer in this jungle was Anton Corbijn, a photographer who has worked with Jagger many times. In photo shoots he would play with the various aspects of the star's mercurial, impudent and utterly unabashed personality. Make-up and masks suited Jagger like no one else, and Corbijn used them for a series of sensational black and white images in which he captured a mysterious and wild Bacchanalian divinity: a devil. Its subject, the man who sang 'Sympathy for the Devil', is a figure who has bowled over more than one generation with his non-conformist and rebellious power.

Following pages **Peter Gabriel** GUIDO HARARI, 1983

Mick Jagger of The Rolling Stones ANTON CORBIJN, 1994

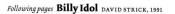

Following pages **Billy Idol** DAVID STRICK, 1991

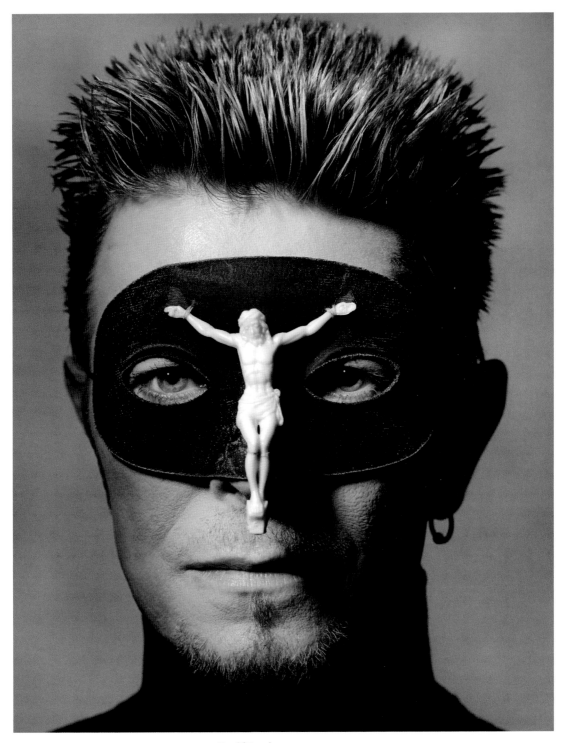

David Bowie ALBERT WATSON, 1996

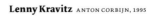

Lenny Kravitz ANTON CORBIJN, 1995

DEMETRIO STRATOS

'My machine gun is a double bass shooting in your face what I think about life.' These are lyrics from 'Gioia e rivoluzione' (joy and revolution), one of the best-known songs by Area. This experimental Italian group, founded by Demetrio Stratos in 1972, used music as the language of struggle and consciousness. The lyrics reflect how Stratos felt during the turbulent 1970s in Italy: 'The voice in music today is a channel of communication which no longer communicates anything,' he wrote in his 1979 essay, 'Diplofonie ed altro' (diplophonies and more). In his work with Area, and throughout in his personal studies his collaborations with John Cage, Andy Warhol and Merce Cunningham, Demetrio Stratos developed the expressive potential of the human voice as few others have done.

Stratos was a naturalized Italian citizen, born of Greek parents in Alexandria, Egypt, and lived right in the heart of Mediterranean culture with all its ethnic diversity and vibrant musical traditions. He studied the techniques of, and importance given to, the voice in the cultures of the Far and Middle East. He also turned his own throat into a laboratory for exploring the limits of the human voice. His vocal cords were superb: Stratos was able to produce polyphonies and to emit sound at a frequency almost beyond the limit of the human voice. All these achievements, he claimed, were only a matter of study and experimentation.

But it was a matter of politics too. Demetrio's voice vibrated in a powerful way, and was filled with the desire for change, the creation of something new and the destruction of dogma. In the sleeve notes to his album *Metrodora* he wrote: 'The vocal overdevelopment of the West has rendered the modern singer almost insensible to all the different aspects of the voice, boxing it into the limited space of certain linguistic structures. It is now even more difficult to shake it out of its process of mummification and drag it out of the privileged and institutionalized expressive traditions belonging to the culture of the ruling classes.'

Demetrio Stratos GUIDO HARARI, 1976

Corey Taylor, Slipknot TIM MOSENFELDER, 2001

Michael Stipe, R.E.M. DAVE M. BENETT, 2005

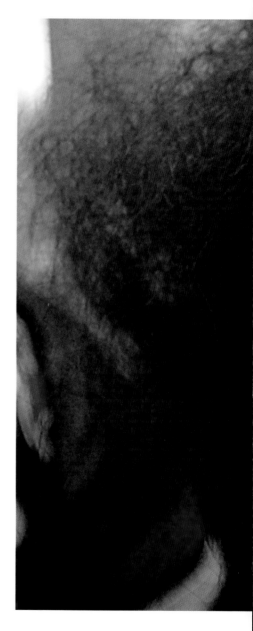

Björk JIM WATSON, 2003

THE
RESIDENTS

The Residents are certainly one of the most mysterious and obscure ensemble in the history of rock music. They have based their whole experimental aesthetic on enigmas: their playing is obscure, their lyrics are obscure and even the musicians are obscured. The little that is known about them has probably been invented, but it is certain that the band formed in San Francisco in the early 1970s. They are opposed to any form of hero worship, and never appear in public without surreal and bizarre masks, such as enormous eyeball helmets. This obscurity was a celebration of their independence from commercial pressures and the music industry at large.

Once British guitarist Philip Lithman (whose stage name was Snakefinger) became part of their outfit, The Residents' own independent label, Ralph Records, was born. In 1974 they released *Meet the Residents*, their first album. The release coincided with the continuing decline of the hippie and acid rock movements, but preceded new wave. Indeed, when it erupted, new wave began to celebrate The Residents as the prophets of a novel way of creating music and performing.

Their method is one of satire and collage. Parodies of music and costumes intended for mass consumption are worked into musical montages comprised of multiple fragments. This produces a tangled web of sounds, which inhabit an atmosphere that feels rough and amateurish. Their multi-mediality, concept albums and similar experiments have made them one of the most radical groups of the musical avant-garde. Some people believe that two famous rock geniuses in particular hide behind The Residents' masks. Such legends are part of the cult, and an air of mystery still clings to The Residents today.

Snakefinger and The Residents RESIDENTS IMAGES, 1986

Grace Jones ROBERT MAPPLETHORPE, 1984

Alice Cooper EVERETT COLLECTION, 1970S

Gene Simmons, KISS BARRY SCHULTZ, 1975

CARMEN MIRANDA

The real name of the lady with the tutti-frutti hat was Maria do Carmo Miranda da Cunha. She was born near Porto in Portugal, but became one of the principal figures of South American exoticism.

At the start of the twentieth century, when she was less than a year old, Carmen Miranda emigrated with her family to Brazil. As the young girl grew up in Rio de Janeiro, she quickly developed a great enthusiasm for the samba. She would show off her talents and ear for music at countryside fiestas and built a name for herself as a dancer and singer, becoming the perfect incarnation of the carefree spirit of that fabulous land.

Broadway and Hollywood turned her into the 'Brazilian Bombshell', and her trademark style involved a mixture of homespun eccentricity, a flamboyant nature, sexual promise and *joie de vivre*. Carmen conquered America as no other performer from South America had ever done before, appearing in stage in musicals like *That Night in Rio* or *The Gang's All Here*. In each performance her flamboyant costumes (often consisting of hats made from various fruits precariously balanced) were matched by her dazzling smile and melodious voice. The tone of the latter was perfect for light-hearted songs like *Chica Chica Boom Chic* or *South American Way*.

Behind the mask, reality was something else entirely. The lady with the tutti-frutti hat struggled with addiction to drugs, alcohol and amphetamines, substances that likely brought about a heart attack at the age of 46. Everyone today, however, still remembers her feathers and hats as the embodiment of the luxurious, *dolce vita* lifestyle of the tropics.

Carmen Miranda ARCHIVIO GBB, 1941

Liberace BOB LEAFE, 1985

The Village People EVERETT COLLECTION, 1980S

Boy George MARK STEWART, 2002

Ben Onono DERRICK SANTINI, 2008

Frank Zappa with his children LYNN GOLDSMITH, 1988

Got no deeds to do / No promises to keep / I'm dappled and drowsy and ready to sleep / Let the morningtime drop all its petals on me / Life, I love you / All is groovy Simon and Garfunkel

Elvis Presley
GIANCOLOMBO, 1958

Bob Marley and Chico Buarque 1980

 **O WHAT IS** everyday life like for an artist? Is it something real, or a collection of illusions? Do the celebrities of the music world do things just like everyone else? Perhaps, or perhaps not. We can, however, say with certainty that normality (whatever *that* is) would be an ambitious goal for some stars; the everyday is an elusive chimera, to which they can only construct wistful elegies.

One of Lou Reed's best loved songs is entitled 'Perfect Day'. It is about nothing more than a walk in the park, just a quiet ordinary day when it was possible to be 'someone else, someone good', this is a normality which has acquired a value because it is something entirely different to a rock 'n' roll life. For a rock star, the value of such a mundane life is its very normally. Pink Floyd even wrote masterpieces on the idea of ordinariness and pleasing little routines, explaining in that solemn assertion from the *Dark Side of the Moon*: 'Us and them / And after all, we're only ordinary men' – lines at the very heart of the most ambitious existential production ever attempted by any rock band.

Lots of artists disguise themselves; they grow moustaches and wear enormous hats in order to feel the thrill of going out and buying a newspaper or a loaf of bread, just like any normal citizen of the world. In fact it can be endearing when the photographer's lens captures a celebrity playing hula hoop, reading stories to their children or playing football (as Bob Marley did whenever he found the space, sometimes even backstage at concerts). The Beatles

The Beatles with Maharishi Mahesh Yogi
KEYSTONE PICTURES, 1967

Simon Le Bon of Duran Duran MARK SHENLEY, 1997

David Bowie and Iman
TERRY O'NEILL, 2000

created a monument to an ordinary day with 'A Day in the Life'. It is one of their greatest works – a song that starts with a man reading a newspaper and then ventures into a metaphysical world. There is a rude awakening in the middle when, suddenly, another man gets out of bed, has breakfast, goes out onto the street. When Simon and Garfunkel described their idea of an ordinary day, they sounded like two dreamy boys skipping school, wanting only to count the cracks between the paving stones on the sidewalk. Frank Zappa, the greatest debunker of all, released a photograph of himself seated comfortably on a toilet. What could be more normal than that? Even Major Tom in 'Space Oddity' who, far from being an astronaut lost in space, was, as Bowie later revealed, just a poor drug addict. And Syd Barrett created impossible journeys that starting with little episodes in his own everyday life. Perhaps the question is not 'can successful artists have normal lives', but rather, 'if you have a normal life, can you become a successful artist?'

Midge Ure, Ultravox DAVID CORIO, 1981

Louis Armstrong DENNIS STOCK, 1958

The Beach Boys
EVERETT COLLECTION, 1978

Elvis and Priscilla Presley with their daughter Lisa Marie EVERETT COLLECTION, 1968

Jerry Lee Lewis and his wife Myra EVERETT COLLECTION, 1958

DUKE ELLINGTON

Duke Ellington led the famous Cotton Club Orchestra in the late 1920s and early 30s. It was his musicians that drew large, mixed black and white audiences to the well-known nightclub in Harlem. Igor Stravinsky made his way there as soon as he arrived New York in order to hear Ellington's magnificent jazz symphonies. George Gershwin could often be found at the club too; he worshipped Duke and confessed that he would have given almost anything to have been the creator of a recording like 'Sophisticated Lady'.

Ellington was one of the greatest jazz composers in history, and his music reflected the diversity of Harlem. 'Sometimes I wonder', he wrote towards the end of his career in *Music Is My Mistress* 'what my music would sound like today had I not been exposed to the sounds and overall climate created by all the wonderful, and very sensitive and soulful people who were the singers, dancers, musicians and actors in Harlem when I first came there'. From the tables of the Cotton Club, Ellington's music and fame grew until they resounded through the most illustrious theatres of New York, and then of Europe and, finally, throughout the whole world. His famous suites, like *Black, Brown and Beige* and *My People*, speak of the lives of black people and the innovative power of their music.

Duke Ellington composed wherever he was: travelling from one concert to another, aboard ship on his way to Europe, or even on the telephone. His son, Mercer, recalled in an interview in 1974: 'The old man was always a showman. When he was working on a project, he'd have somebody taking off this part of it, while he had another thing going on this side, and everybody who was only handling a piece of it would wonder how was he ever going to finish it....I think the people who worked on the A-bomb learned their modus operandi from Duke Ellington! All of a sudden, it would all gel right before your eyes. A half hour before the performance of My People, he had one part being done in New York and another in Chicago!' The old showman was able to create entirely personal and unique music using the voices of his orchestra. On the occasion of his seventy-fifth birthday, when illness forced him to stay in a hospital bed, he was deluged with good wishes from the entire world of jazz. Miles Davis paid tribute, saying: 'I think all the musicians in jazz should get together on one certain day and get down on their knees to thank Duke.'

Duke Ellington KEYSTONE PICTURES, 1958

Dizzy Gillespie GIUSEPPE PINO, 1975

Van Morrison and his wife Janet ELLIOTT LANDY, 1969

Preceding pages **The Jackson Five** LAWRENCE SCHILLER, LATE 1960S

George Harrison of The Beatles TERRY O'NEILL, 1975

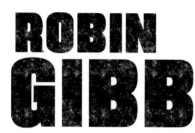

ROBIN GIBB

Robin Gibb always seems to have had a great passion for history, and it was precisely this passion that led the singer-songwriter for the Bee Gees to buy his house, Thame Park, a thirteenth-century monastery in Oxfordshire. 'The Bishops decided Joan of Arc's fate in the chapel here. Henry VIII and Anne Boleyn stayed here in 1533 on one of their progresses. Oh, and Baroness Sophie Wenham conducted her affair with William IV here' Robin Gibb told an interviewer. 'There's a very old set of stone steps outside that the Baroness used to climb into her carriage. She was short. [My wife] Dwina uses them now to climb into the Range Rover. I like that kind of continuity, too: the melding of the old and the new.' When the house came up for sale Mick Jagger was the first to view it, and he fell hopelessly in love with the place. Its owner, however, wouldn't sell it to him: he refused to countenance rock stars and their wild parties. But Gibb's passion for history and his considerable knowledge about the events of England's past impressed the reluctant owner so much that he managed to convince him to accept his offer. That isn't all that is interesting about Gibb's beautiful home: the former monastery seems to be inhabited by other, less well-behaved residents, particularly the ghost of a gardener who likes to play tricks on the family. As Robin told *The Daily Record*: 'There's even a resident ghost, who mysteriously fills up the water in the old font in the chapel, which we converted into a dining room.' A perfectly normal domestic arrangement for a pop star who sang: 'The ghost is waiting outside' at the end of the 1980s on 'Giving Up The Ghost'.

Robin Gibb of The Bee Gees NICK WILSON, 2007

**The wedding of Ringo
Starr and Barbara Bach**

TERRY O'NEILL, 1981

Following pages **Bob Dylan and his son Jesse** ELLIOTT LANDY, 1968

Roger Daltry of The Who TERRY O'NEILL, 1978

BOB DYLAN

Bob Dylan is a poet, a prophet, a revolutionary, an enigma. He is continuously elusive, and displays the perpetually riddling nature of a sphinx. As he says: 'All I can do is be me, whoever that is.' Born Robert Allen Zimmerman, this young man decided at the age of 19 to give himself a new name, one that would mark a developing identity, a new life and a new history. Ever since he has been in perpetual contradiction with the image everyone else had of him, and still rejects every attempt made – even by photographers – to define him in a particular pose. The cigarette dangling from his lips or slim fingers is perhaps the only element that has remained constant since those early years. That and his disquieting and evasive gaze.

Bob Dylan had an incredible capacity for changing both his shape and appearance, as folk singer Eric Von Schmidt remembers: 'The whole time he was in London, he wore the same thing, his blue jeans and cap. And sometimes he would look big and muscular, and the next day he'd look like a little gnome, and one day he'd be kind of handsome and virile, and the following day he'd look like a thirteen-year-old child.' He was as protean as his voice. When Dylan arrived in New York in 1961, he was as thin as a pencil and had a head filled dreams of a musical life as sincere as that of Woody Guthrie. Greenwich Village, its streets still echoing with the civil rights movement, became his home and in a short time he conquered it all. No one else in the history of music has been so admired and held in such unanimous esteem: from Jimi Hendrix to Keith Richards, from Patti Smith to John Lennon, Dylan has made an impression on them all.

Back then, the times really were a-changing, and Dylan condensed his generation's yearning into his folk ballads, which he delivered with a rock attitude. The protest movement chose him as their spokesman, but Dylan's type of protest was never limited to any one plan of political activism. He became restless, dropped out and in 'Maggie's Farm' sang: 'Well, I try my best to be just like I am / But everybody wants you to be just like them.'

As Dylan's musical career progressed, he became both more subversive and more profound. The artist stopped dressing as a working folk-singer, and adopted a more rock appearance, which included black jackets, dark glasses and boots. His music underwent a similar change, moving from protest songs, through his 'electric conversion' to a new language of rock that drew on the work of poets such as Rimbaud, Poe and T. S. Eliot. In 1965, Dylan's tour of Britain was filmed for the documentary, *Don't Look Back*. He found that his acoustic set had become a boring ritual in which he no longer recognized himself, and he felt ready to leave behind all the old certainties and throw the shattering invective of 'Like a Rolling Stone' in his audience's faces.

Bob Dylan BARRY FEINSTEIN, 1966

Chris Stein and Debbie Harry of Blondie LYNN GOLDSMITH, 1978

Creedence Clearwater Revival EVERETT COLLECTION, 1970S

Following pages **Sonny & Cher** IVAN NAGY, 1965

Sammy Davis Jr FRANK DANDRIDGE, 1964

Yves Montand and Simone Signoret EVE ARNOLD, 1966

ROBERT PLANT

The strength of Robert Plant's voice was nowhere better exhibited than in the primal battle cry at the start of the 'Immigrant Song'; the powerful vocals seemed to come directly from the throats of the Viking hordes mentioned in the song. Led Zeppelin's lead singer cultivated a wild image, and with that mane of curly blond hair he looked half rocker, half hippie. Plant wore figure-hugging clothes, had an uninhibited and provocative attitude on stage, and his extreme vocal range allowed him to switch from a sob to a scream in an instant. All these attributes have made him an icon for singers in almost every rock and hard-rock band that have existed since.

The group's enormous success following their first two albums meant that in a short time this raw, bluesy singer from the Midlands in England had metamorphosed into a global sex symbol, living a rock star life on the road. The touring was endless, luxurious hotel rooms were wrecked and there were vast screaming crowds everywhere. 'We liked living on the edge' said the band's guitarist Jimmy Page. 'It was a way of feeding the music.' When working on their third album, however, Led Zeppelin decided to allow themselves a moment's rest, and took a creative break in the countryside; they went to Bron-Yr-Aur, an isolated cottage in the lush mountains of Snowdonia in Wales. Jimmy Page and Robert Plant were studying the roots of their British culture. They were looking back, towards folk music, towards a new – less electric – sound. Jimmy Page remembers: 'Robert and I went to Bron-Yr-Aur in 1970. We'd been working solidly right up to that point. Even recordings were done on the road. We had this time off and Robert suggested the cottage. I certainly hadn't been to that area of Wales. So we took our guitars down there and played a few bits and pieces. This wonderful countryside, panoramic views and having the guitars...it was just an automatic thing to be playing. And we started writing.'

Robert Plant of Led Zeppelin RANDOLPH, 1970

Joe Cocker VIENNA REPORT, 1984

Grace Slick SAM FALK, 1970

Billy Joel DAMON WINTER, 2008

Count Basie with his wife Catherine Morgan GUY LE QUERREC, 1980

Serge Gainsbourg BRUNO BARBEY, 1966

Following pages **Pink Floyd** NIK WHEELER, 1974

Ronnie Wood and his wife Krissie TERRY O'NEILL, 1975

Joan Baez (left) with her sisters Pauline and Mimi Lagarde 1960s

Tom Jones

TONY FRANK, 1966

Phil Collins with his mother June DAVID CHANCELLOR, 2003

Johnny Cash JAN PERSSON, 1971

Dizzy Gillespie HERB RITTS, 1989

EVERY LITTLE THING

Every little thing she does is magic / Every thing she do just turns me on / Even though my life before was tragic / Now I know my love for her goes on The Police

The Strokes ANDY COTTERILL, 1999

N THE FAMOUS music video for 'We Are the World' the camera starts low down with a pair of shiny shoes and carefully folded white socks, as it rises we catch a glimpse of a white glove on the right hand, and only on the right hand. Before the camera has reached the subject's face we already know that we are looking at Michael Jackson – such is the power of details. It is the same when we see Keith Richards's bent fingers covered with pirate rings, or Miles Davis's trumpet, the pink curves of Prince's guitar, Dizzy Gillespie's puffed-out cheeks, Louis Armstrong's chapped lips, or even just one of Willie Nelson's wrinkles. There are times when they transcend their lowly position and become icons in themselves: small parts can represent the whole. Photography employs the power of a microscope as it investigates, probing, enlarging, allowing us to discover a whole universe that would otherwise have remained closed to us. If the devil really is in the details, then the photographer will find him.

Charles Mingus GIUSEPPE PINO, 1975

Amy Winehouse BRYAN ADAMS, 2007

Ozzy Osbourne ANDREW WINNING, 2009

Music, when seen through this magnifying glass, is a limitless construct of details: a plectrum striking the strings of a guitar, a slider moving up and down, a breath of air between mouth and a microphone, the sound made by the keys of a saxophone, a stray strand of hair, a spiral of smoke, a handkerchief wiping away sweat, fingers forcefully hitting the keys of a piano. Sometimes such details can symbolize a musician's whole career. Indeed, the whole vast show of *The Wall* could be summed up by that one disjointed little pink doll thrown into a corner at the foot of an imposing wall of white bricks. Neil Young, in one of his famous and extraordinary stage sets, placed fake amplifiers and strange-looking microphones on stage in order to emphasize every detail of these mediating devices through which the music would flow. Just as in *Gulliver's Travels*, it is sometimes enough to reverse the proportions, making something large that we would normally see as small, in order for us to understand just how important certain details really are, and how music couldn't do without them.

Ella Fitzgerald
ALBUM, 1971

LOUIS ARMSTRONG

'If anybody was Mr. Jazz it was Louis Armstrong' said Duke Ellington after the famous trumpeter's death. 'He was the epitome of jazz and always will be.' Moreover, in the second half of the 1920s, Armstrong was the first to raise African American music from the Deep South of the United States to the level of art. Louis came from the poorest part of New Orleans, where friends called him Dipper, because his mouth was shaped like a ladle. During a stay at reform school that lasted a year and half he began playing the trumpet, and ended up conducting the band. Life was hard in New Orleans, but not for too long. America soon began to take notice of Armstrong, and New York and Chicago were quick to welcome and fall in love with the young trumpeter.

The cornetist Rex Stewart remembered Armstrong's arrival in New York: 'I went mad with the rest of the town. I tried to walk like him, talk like him, eat like him, sleep like him. I even bought a pair of big policeman shoes like he used to wear and stood outside his apartment waiting for him to come out so I could look at him.' For Armstrong, 1928 was a golden year when, among other pieces, he recorded 'West End Blues', one of the masterpieces in the history of jazz. His music is both simple and solemn, and as exhilarating as his deep, hoarse voice. His was the most famous mouth in jazz, but it was often punished by lengthy tours. He loved to play to the gallery and was an entertainer with a great talent for mimicry, but, above all, he was the musician who changed the course of American music. When he died, thousands came to pay their last respects in New York and New Orleans, and the *New York Times* wrote that if jazz was the USA's greatest contribution to the art of the world, it was Louis Armstrong that should be thanked.

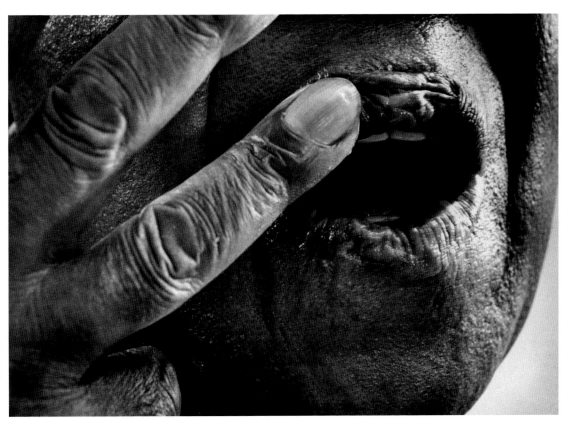

Louis Armstrong JOHN LOENGARD, 1965

Little Richard BARON WOLMAN, 1969

Bob Marley EVERETT COLLECTION, 1970S

SINÉAD O'CONNOR

Shaving her head seems to have been her first gesture of protest against the pressures and intrusions of the media, and her bald head became her most enduring symbol. Sinéad O'Connor's provocative behaviour – sometimes bordering on desperate rebellion – contributed to her fame, but has also caused outrage on occasion. Her 1987 debut album, *The Lion and the Cobra*, was very striking: this 20-year-old Irish girl, shaven-headed, almost androgynous but with large doe eyes, had an acrobatic voice, capable of expressing in turn tenderness and quivering rage. Her childhood had been far from easy, yet she was able to express her emotions with a visceral intensity.

Her second album, *I Do Not Want What I Haven't Got*, was hugely successful all over the world, and the first hit album of the 1990s. *Rolling Stone* magazine decided to award her the title 'artist of the year', and dedicated the cover of their March 1991 issue to her. They called in Herb Ritts, one of the greatest contemporary photographers, to take the pictures of her. The secret of his vision and his images was naturalness and a deep sensibility. 'This photograph', he recalled, 'was taken down at my beach house in Malibu one afternoon for *Rolling Stone*. She had not a stitch of make-up on, and obviously nobody to do her hair. There was such a weight to her, almost like she was a sculpture, angelic and heavy at the same time.' Ritts asked her to rest her head against a wall and close her eyes, making this profile, taken in black and white, even more solemn. He then turned the image by 90 degrees to made it look as if that rebel neck was lying down, as if she were being allowed a moment of silent repose.

Sinéad O'Connor HERB RITTS, 1990

Roy Ayres GIUSEPPE PINO, 1969

Seal PHIL KNOTT, 2000

Lily Allen DERRICK SANTINI, 2006

ZZ Top SIMONE CECCHETTI, 2010

Stevie Wonder GUIDO HARARI, 1981

Willie Nelson THEO WARGO, 2003

ERIC CLAPTON

Graffiti declaring 'Clapton is God' first appeared on walls in London in 1966. He had only one rival for the role of guitar god, and that was his friend Jimi Hendrix, whose death affected Clapton deeply. He subsequently opened all of his concerts in that unhappy year of 1970 with 'Little Wing' as a tribute to Hendrix. Nicknamed 'Slowhand', Clapton lent an air of distinction to bands with his mere presence; he played with The Yardbirds, The Bluesbreakers, Cream, and Blind Faith before becoming a solo artist in the middle of the 1970s. His career and personal life have been a roller coaster of meltdowns and recoveries, punctuated by drug addiction and an accident that caused the death of his son, Conor.

In this extreme close-up of Clapton's face, Guido Harari has caught a drop of sweat (but it could just as easily be a tear). With his eyes almost closed, Slowhand is playing the instrumental coda that ends 'Layla', one of his most emotional songs. Clapton had begun to explore the potential of the electric guitar with Cream in the middle of the 1960s. He then dispensed with every frill, every magic trick, virtuosity and experimentation simply to play his instrument, and return to the emotional nature of the blues. Some fans were angry with him, but most continued to worship the god who sang 'Cocaine'.

Eric Clapton GUIDO HARARI, 1987

Ozzy Osbourne CLAUDIA RORARIUS, 2007

Johnny Cash's guitar STEPHEN CHERNIN, 2004

Buck Clayton GIUSEPPE PINO, 1975

Helen Humes GIUSEPPE PINO, 1974

Courtney Love WENDY HU, 2010

AXL ROSE

With his tattoos, long hair, angelic face, screaming voice, model figure and dissolute lifestyle, the Guns N' Roses singer Axl Rose has built up a huge following of fans, from little girls to hardened metalheads. When he sang 'Welcome to the Jungle' he was talking about Los Angeles in the 1980s, but also specifically about his own wild lifestyle. He recalled in an interview with *Rolling Stone* that his difficult childhood was marked by frequent abuse, and then came rock, women and heroin. His tattoos became his costume, and the black rose which stands out on his right shoulder appears on the cover of the Thin Lizzy album *Black Rose: A Rock Legend*. Immediately below the black rose is the face of the woman for whom, according to legend, Axl wrote 'Don't Cry'. Finally, on the same arm is the design for the cover of their first album, *Appetite for Destruction*, in which the Guns' faces are transformed into skulls set on a cross.

Herb Ritts was fascinated by the contrast of form and image, and the atmosphere of his portraits hovers between the sensuality of Axl's lips and the macabre look of his arms. The photo session was scheduled so that the cover of *Rolling Stone* would coincide with the release of the band's second album, *Use Your Illusion*, in 1991. The appointment was set for nine in the evening and the session was planned to last a couple of hours. Axl Rose turned up six hours late. Despite the short time available to them Herb Ritts remembered 'Axl kept changing clothes on the set. You just could not resist, you know. His lips and his form, and the fact that he had those symbolic tattoos. It was pretty amazing.' The session ended at six in the morning and produced some of the most iconic and sensual images of the Guns N' Roses singer.

Axl Rose, Guns N' Roses HERB RITTS, 1991

Johnny Hallyday TONY FRANK, 1995

MICHAEL JACKSON

On 25 March 1983, a television special celebrated 25 years of Motown, the record label that had released the Jackson Five's debut. During that special, after singing 'I'll Be There' with his brothers, Michael Jackson appeared on stage wearing a black, sequined jacket, a black hat and, on his left hand, one white glove covered in rhinestones. He performed solo, singing 'Billie Jean' and for the first time showed the whole world his ultra-famous moonwalk. The charismatic performance was seen by millions of viewers, and the event was unlike anything since Elvis Presley or The Beatles had appeared on the *Ed Sullivan Show*. His style of singing and dancing was quite overwhelming, and from then on this costume was to become his trademark. Jacko dressed the same way for all his later performances of the song.

The story of Michael Jackson is a remarkable one. He rocketed from child prodigy to global superstar, and was along the way deeply affected by celebrity and excess. He became a tragic figure in his last years, when – tormented by legal trials and the paparazzi – bouts of plastic surgery left him with a barely recognizable face. At the height of his career, however, Jackson was indisputably the King of Pop and the greatest star in the world. He sold a billion albums, and *Thriller* was the highest-selling album of all time. The 1980s danced and sang to his music.

Even Michael Jackson's death became a spectacle, with millions of viewers on television and the internet watching the public memorial service in the Staples Center, Los Angeles. In November 2009, his black fedora hat and white glove were sold at auction for, of course, record-breaking prices – just like everything else connected to His Royal Highness, the King of Pop.

Following pages **A video of Michael Jackson** JAMES VEYSEY, 2009

Michael Jackson's glove and hat UPI, 2010

Graffiti on the wall of Abbey Road Studios in London FELIX CLAY, 2009

ALL AROUND THE WORLD

All around the world, you've got to spread the word / Tell them what you heard / We're gonna make a better day / All around the world, You've got to spread the word / Tell them what you heard / You know it's gonna be ok

Oasis

Celebrating John Lennon's birthday at the Strawberry Fields memorial in New York KEITH BEDFORD, 2010

AST OF ALL, let's take a journey, a tour, in search of the world's music. Having looked at details, guitars, masks, hats, eyes, stages and backstage areas, all that's left is to look at the places where all-pervasive music has appeared around the world. The short answer is 'everywhere'. Though music is invisible, and impossible to quantify, it covers our planet. After more than a century, the new media have succeeded in multiplying, spreading and turning music into an omnipresent soundtrack for the people of the world. Music follows, attracts and hypnotizes us everywhere we go. On the other hand, music also attaches itself to specific places, making them its own and marking them forever. Graffiti is tirelessly scrawled onto the wall of the Abbey Road Studios; fresh flowers are placed each day on the graves of dead musical heroes; the skylines of cities remind us of songs.

We could travel forever following the footprints that music has left in the streets, paying our respects in provincial bars, parks and museums – all shrines to the memory of certain songs. We could also tour the homes of music's great kings: Elvis's home, Graceland, where even the front gates are designed to resemble a musical score; or Michael Jackson's Neverland

Hard Rock Cafe in Las Vegas
VEGAS 5, 2010

Tango dancers ALBUM, 2002

Busker on the New York Subway BRUCE DAVIDSON, 1980

Ranch, the name evoking thoughts of freedom and perpetual happiness. The search for the places marked by music could take us to theatres, arenas, vast fields; places where the vibrations of collective explosions still resonate. In some remote places, the links with music are kept alive only by dedicated fans, guardians who will not allow the sacred flame to die.

It is not just in places that music leaves a trace; it also leaves its marks on the faces and lifestyles of those who love it. Music dictates certain behaviours and fashions, and generates imitators. Even in the fading dreams of those who tried but never quite made it; the traces of music endure.

THE ISLE OF

WIGHT

In late August 1970, East Afton Farm on the Isle of Wight was the setting for what was perhaps the last great event of the epic era that had begun in 1967 with the Summer of Love. That summer about 600,000 people arrived on the island in the English Channel – an impressive number of visitors for a patch of land that had approximately 100,000 inhabitants.

Tents and lots of hair shared the green, open fields, while the stage was filled with great acts: including Miles Davis, Jimi Hendrix and Jim Morrison. In between, there were also performances by Joan Baez, Leonard Cohen, Emerson, Lake & Palmer, Jethro Tull, Kris Kristofferson and The Who, to name just a few.

Jimi Hendrix took to the stage at about midnight, opening with a distorted version of 'God Save The Queen'. Though he couldn't have known it, the Isle of Wight festival was to be his last big concert, and he played with a savage grace, giving it everything he could give. It was also the last European appearance for The Doors and Jim Morrison. The 1960s, with all its dreams of freedom and protests for peace, was now leaving the field open to the coming decade, which would have a very different flavour.

Less than a month after the gig Hendrix was found dead in a hotel room, having overdosed on barbiturates; Janis Joplin, another icon of freedom, died in a Hollywood motel in October 1970; and Jim Morrison also died a year later in his home in Paris. All this was to come, but for a brief period in August on that island in the Channel, music was still the perfect adhesive for a social movement of youth protest. Art, life, rock, politics, dreams and non-conformism were held together by the power and energy of a collective ritual.

Previous pages **A Beatles anniversary at Abbey Road** DWAYNE SENIOR, 2009

The Isle of Wight Festival FAUSTO GIACCARO, 1970

The Cavern in Liverpool, the club where The Beatles debuted KEYSTONE PICTURES, 1960S

Beatles fans outside Buckingham Palace in London CENTRAL PRESS, 1965

Traditional folk music at McSorley's Old Ale House in New York BURT GLINN, 1959

A New Orleans jazz band DENNIS STOCK, 1958

THE JUKEBOX

This is it, one of the symbols of popular American culture. It sits in the corner of a bar and has pride of place in the imagination of more than one generation. The jukebox is a fantastic object that can seemingly transport listeners through time. A coin is all it takes for the sounds of smoke-filled bars in the Roaring Twenties to crackle and play from this machine of dreams.

In our collective memory, the jukebox is most often associated with rock 'n' roll, even though the swing era was its true golden period (when the revenue it drew helped to protect the music of artists such as Glenn Miller). After swing came the blues, and it wasn't long before the 'Devil's music' could be heard in bars. Most especially the bars of Chicago.

Workers arriving from Dixie at the end of the 1940s brought a new music to the Windy City, songs and tunes that contained the history and testament of black people. From there, the blues travelled throughout the land, leaving it touched and enriched. The history of slavery and the suffering of a whole people entered bars, walked along the country's streets, passed through a jukebox and became part of a nation's history.

A blues bar in Chicago BRUCE DAVIDSON, 1962

The Notting Hill Carnival in London CHRIS STEELE PERKINS, 1975

An Afro-Cuban music concert GUY LE QUERREC, 2001

THE SEX PISTOLS

'We're the flowers in the dustbin, we're the poison in your human machine, we're the future, your future', yelled the Sex Pistols on their second single, 'God Save the Queen'. For both London and New York, 1977 was a flashpoint: an angry young generation was ready for a new language at precisely the time when the destructive fury of punk came bursting out.

The provocative behaviour punk encouraged was a revolt against the boring respectability of bourgeois society, and against the preceding generation of protesters. The message of peace and love from the 1960s now seemed tired and outdated. And if the lyrics of punk songs and attitude on stage were outrageous, then their outfits and lifestyles were even more so. They did away with long hair and flowery skirts, and brought in a new aesthetic of violently clashing clothes. Punk stole objects from other countercultures and refashioned them.

At the heart of this stylistic revolution was 430 King's Road, London, where in 1971 the young Vivienne Westwood set up her first shop, Let it Rock, with her partner Malcolm McLaren. In 1972 the shop changed its name and became Too Fast to Live, Too Young to Die; in 1974 it was renamed Sex; and then in 1976 it became Seditionaries, reflecting a new provocative and shocking strategy of stealing from the aesthetics of fetish and sadomasochism. King's Road became the spiritual home of the punk scene, and Vivienne Westwood created pieces that swiftly became cult objects: tight trousers and T-shirts often decorated with studs, rips, zips, chains, safety pins and crucifixes. It was near the shop that Steve Jones, guitarist of the Strand saw Johnny Rotten (otherwise known as John Lydon) with his hair dyed green and a T-shirt with 'I hate Pink Floyd' written on it. Rotten soon joined the group and the Sex Pistols were born. McLaren, by then their manager, dressed them head to toe in clothes designed by Westwood. It was this period that established the profitable relationship between music and fashion that continues today.

Vivienne Westwood in her London boutique, Seditionaries DENNIS MORRIS, 1977

Jazz band in the French Quarter of New Orleans THOMAS HOEPKER, 1991

Chris Carrabba of Dashboard Confessional at CBGB, the birthplace of punk in New York ALYSON ALIANO, 2003

**Famous guitars
on display at
Harrods in London**

RICHARD STONEHOUSE, 2007

JIMI HENDRIX

Jimi Hendrix's legendary Fender Stratocaster is one of the jewels around which the museum of rock in Seattle is built. That guitar, which came howling into the history of Western culture, has become immortal and *Are You Experienced*, the astounding first album by the Jimi Hendrix Experience, has its title paralleled in the museum's name: The Experience Music Project. In 2000 the project opened its doors to a city that has been particularly fertile ground for rock – it is the birthplace not only of Hendrix, but also Nirvana, Pearl Jam, Foo Fighters and Alice in Chains. The entrance to the museum is filled with an enormous interactive sculpture, *Roots and Branches*, created by the artist Trimpin. It is a tornado of about 500 instruments, mostly electric guitars, which are controlled by a computer to play together automatically.

In 1995, the Rock and Roll Hall of Fame and Museum opened in Cleveland, Ohio. The musical and cultural revolution of rock is now, it seems, being placed in museums in an attempt to immortalize the music and the musicians that changed the world, influencing the dress and lifestyles of generations.

The museum of a revolution can do no more than display its heirlooms and its memorabilia. That famous guitar is given the space it deserves in the Seattle museum, and the Guitar Gallery there is dedicated to the everlasting memory of Hendrix, one of the greatest guitarists of all time.

The Experience Music Project in Seattle CHRISTIAN HEEB, 2008

Elvis impersonator Miguel Olivares-Alvarez DAVE YOUNG, 2009

Amy Winehouse impersonator Danielle Merrick DAVE YOUNG, 2009

Elvis memorabilia on sale in London JAMES VEYSEY, 1999

Items that belonged to Michael Jackson on show in Beverly Hills before the 2009 auction EZIO PETERSEN, 2009

VALÉRIE BELIN

All stars that there have ever been – both great and small – have had lookalikes. There are hosts of Elvis Presleys, Michael Jacksons and Madonnas filling our streets and clubs. If people can't have the original, then they can at least have a copy.

When a star becomes an icon, his or her image crystallizes into certain key features, allowing it to be endlessly reproduced. Such identification can produce both impressive and grotesque results. The history of music is filled with the histories of imitators, some of whom have approached legendary status. One such incident is the 'death' of Paul McCartney: so well known that it is often simply referred to as 'PID' (Paul is dead). The story goes that the bassist of The Beatles died in a traffic accident in 1966, and was subsequently replaced by a lookalike. The fact that some fans believed this rumour tells us that by this time the image of an icon had become so reproducible, that nobody could really be sure where the line between imitator and celebrity could be drawn.

Valérie Belin's photographic portraits of various Michael Jackson lookalikes question the very notions of identity and similarity, of reality and illusion: 'One can consider my work an obsessive attempt to appropriate the real, in which "the body" plays a decisive role', wrote the photographer. These 'Jackson' faces look like shop-window manikins as they look into the distance, impersonal and silent. The image is devoid of dramatization, and the photography is stripped of any self-expression.

Michael Jackson impersonator VALÉRIE BELIN, 2003

British Teddy Boys CHRIS STEELE-PERKINS, 1976

Following pages **A pop festival in France** BRUNO BARBEY, 1976

A punk in Stockholm KEYSTONE, 1977

The Strawberry Fields memorial to John Lennon in New York's Central Park MONIKA GRAFF, 2009

The grave of Jim Morrison in the Père Lachaise Cemetery in Paris SUS, 1970S

A photo of Marilyn Manson in a Bishkek nightclub in Kyrgyzstan IGOR STARKOV, 2008

The flag of the Sex Pistols RICHARD STONEHOUSE, 2000

 Elvis died in 1977, but his memory certainly hasn't faded away. On the twentieth anniversary of his death, 70,000 people gathered together at Graceland for the silent Candlelight Vigil: a memorial procession celebrated each year. The legendary Graceland was the King's residence, a regal palace where Elvis lived for twenty years until his death, and where, in his famous Garden of Meditation, he is buried. Every centimetre of the stone walls surrounding the estate along Elvis Presley Boulevard is covered in graffiti and messages. Each year thousands of people on a secular pilgrimage leave their mark on this wall. Some fans weren't even born when Elvis died, but the power of his music and image are enough to draw them to Memphis.

Graceland was opened to the public in 1982, and it is now (after the White House) the most famous and visited residence in the United States. In 1991 it was even declared a National Historic Monument. During Elvis Week, thousands of fans defy the sultry subtropical heat of a Tennessee August and transform Graceland into a temple.

Rock music has to be seen as well as listened to, and it needs identification to create a sense of belonging. Graceland isn't alone on the list of music's sacred places. Even though the numbers are smaller, processions still wind towards the Père Lachaise Cemetery in Paris, where people bow down before the tomb of the Lizard King, Jim Morrison. They leave behind them flowers, poetry, and sometimes even bottles of beer or other offerings. There is also the circular mosaic of the Strawberry Fields Memorial, a garden in Central Park dedicated to John Lennon's memory. In these temples of remembrance people pay homage, ask questions and confide their thoughts as if to a friend. They are there to commune with the divinities of our present age: the immortal, pagan gods of rock 'n' roll. But, then again, can anyone be sure that Jim and Elvis are really dead?

Graffiti at Graceland, the home of Elvis Presley in Memphis DAVID GILES, 2002

Graceland WALTER BIBIKOW, 1999

Graceland WALTER BIBIKOW, 1999

获52届格莱美五项大奖提名
当今音乐流行时尚唯一超人气女神
LADY GAGA 全新EP
LADY GAGA
THE FAME MONSTER
嘎嘎小姐 | 超人气女魔头
收录首周攻占英美排行、称霸全球10国冠军+23国Top 10"Bad Romance"等8首新曲
次波单曲Telephone力邀碧昂丝友情跨刀，两大天后强强联手 打造舞池新热度
赢取Lady Gaga代言的时尚耳机
请登陆http://www.myspace.cn/ladygaga
详情请见专辑内附活动说明
现正全城热卖
LADY GAGA
LADY GAGA
THE FAME MONSTER

Lady Gaga posters in Beijing
STEPHEN SHAVER, 2010

Jeff Mills TANIA RUSSO, 2003

ESSENTIAL DISCOGRAPHY

The list that follows is a personal selection, taken from the music created by some of the artists who have appeared in these pages. Due to reasons of space, only one album has been chosen for each artist. *Gino Castaldo*

Bowie, David – *Heroes*, 1977
Brown, James – *Live at the Apollo*, 1963
Buarque, Cico – *Meus Caros Amigos*, 1976
Buckley, Jeff – *Grace*, 1994
Cash, Johnny – *At Folsom Prison*, 1968
Cave, Nick – *Murder Ballads*, 1996
Charles, Ray – *The Birth of Soul: The Complete Atlantic R&B: 1951–1959*, 1991
Chevalier, Maurice – *Maurice Chevalier: Vol. 1: 1919–1930*, 2000
Christian, Charlie – *Solo Flight: The Genius of Charlie Christian*, 1972
Clapton, Eric – *see* Cream
Cocker, Joe – *With a Little Help from My Friends*, 1969
Cohen, Leonard – *Songs of Leonard Cohen*, 1967
Cole, Nat King – *The Classic Singles*, 2003
Cooper, Alice – *Love it to Death*, 1971
Costello, Elvis – *This Year's Model*, 1978
Cream – *Goodbye Cream*, 1969
Creedence Clearwater Revival – *Green River*, 1969
Crosby, Stills, Nash & Young – *4 Way Street*, 1971
Culture Club – *Colour by Numbers*, 1983
Daft Punk – *Discovery*, 2001
Dashboard Confessional – *The Places You Have Come to Fear the Most*, 2001
Davis, Miles – *Kind of Blue*, 1959
Davis, Jr, Sammy – *The Wham of Sam*, 1961
De Andrè, Fabrizio – *Nuvole*, 1990
Deep Purple – *Made in Japan*, 1972
Depeche Mode – *Violator*, 1990
Doors, The – *The Doors*, 1967
Duran Duran – *Seven and the Ragged Tiger*, 1983
Dylan, Bob – *Highway 61 Revisited*, 1965
Ellington, Duke – *The Indispensable Duke Ellington*, 1961
Eminem – *The Marshall Mathers LP*, 2000
Eno, Brian – *Before and After Science*, 1977
Eurythmics – *Sweet Dreams*, 1983
Evans, Bill – *Conversations with Myself*, 1963
Evora, Cesaria – *Cesaria*, 1995
Faithfull, Marianne – *Broken English*, 1979
Ferry, Bryan – *Boys and Girls*, 1985
Fitzgerald, Ella – *The Cole Porter Songbook*, 1965
Fripp, Robert – *see* King Crimson
Gabriel, Peter – *So*, 1986

Little Richard – *Here's Little Richard*, 1957
Little Steven – *Voice of America*, 1984
Love, Courtney – *see* Hole
McLaughlin, John – *Devotion*, 1970
Madonna – *Like a Virgin*, 1984
Manson, Marilyn – *Antichrist Superstar*, 1996
Marley, Bob (& The Wailers) – *Natty Dread*, 1974
Marsalis, Wynton – *Think of One*, 1983
Metheny, Pat – *American Garage*, 1980
Mingus, Charles – *The Black Saint and the Sinner Lady*, 1963
Minnelli, Liza – *Cabaret*, 1972
Miranda, Carmen – *Carmen Miranda: 1930–1945*, 1997
Mitchell, Joni – *Blue*, 1971
Monk, Thelonious – *Monk's Music*, 1957
Montand, Yves – *Le Paris de...Montand*, 1964
Morrison, Van – *Astral Weeks*, 1968
Nelson, Willie – *Yesterday's Wine*, 1971
Nirvana – *Nevermind*, 1991
Oasis – *(What's the Story) Morning Glory?*, 1995
O'Connor, Sinéad – *I Do Not Want What I Haven't Got*, 1990
Osbourne, Ozzy – *see* Black Sabbath
Pearl Jam – *Ten*, 1991
Piaf, Édith – *Olympia 1961*, 1961
Pink Floyd – *The Dark Side of the Moon*, 1973
Police, The – *Regatta de Blanc*, 1979
Pop, Iggy – *Lust for Life*, 1977
Presley, Elvis – *Elvis Presley*, 1956
Prince – *Sign o' the Times*, 1987
Queen – *A Night at the Opera*, 1975
Ra, Sun – *Heliocentric Worlds of Sun Ra: Vol. 1*, 1965
Radiohead – *OK Computer*, 1997
Ramones – *Ramones*, 1976
Rava, Enrico – *The Pilgrim and the Stars*, 1975
Red Hot Chili Peppers – *Blood Sugar Sex Magik*, 1991
Reed, Lou – *Transformer*, 1972
Reinhardt, Django – *Djangology*, 2005
R.E.M. – *Automatic for the People*, 1992
Residents, The – *Meet the Residents*, 1974
Richard, Cliff – *Cliff's Hit Album*, 1963
Rolling Stones, The – *Let it Bleed*, 1969

Dave Gahan, Depeche Mode COHEN MAGEN, 2009

INDEX OF ARTISTS

Photographers at a Rolling Stones press conference HULTON ARCHIVE, 1969

PHOTOGRAPHY CREDITS

p. 160 (above left) Bettmann/Corbis
(above right and below) Giorgio Lotti/
Contrasto
p. 161 Mick Hutson/Getty Images
p. 163 Dennis Stock/Magnum Photos
p. 164–65 Phil Stern
p. 166 Giuseppe Pino/Contrasto
p. 167 R.A./Gamma-Rapho
p. 169 Dennis Stock/Magnum Photos
p. 170–71 Elliott Landy/Magnum Photos
p. 173 Elliott Landy/Magnum Photos
p. 174 Bettmann/Corbis
p. 175 Jim Marshall © Jim Marshall
Photography LLC
p. 177 RBO/Camera Press
p. 178–79 George Rose/Getty Images
p. 180 Dennis Morris/Camera Press
p. 181 Everett Collection
p. 182–83 Everett Collection
p. 185 Ebet Roberts/Getty Images
p. 186–87 Graham Wiltshire/Camera Press
p. 189 Rob Werhorst/Getty Images
p. 190–91 Luciano Viti/Getty Images
p. 192 Mattia Zoppellaro/Contrasto
p. 193 Louise Stickland
p. 195 Terry O'Neill/Camera Press
p. 196–97 Roger Hutchings/Corbis
p. 199 Neal Preston/Corbis
p. 200 Neal Preston/Corbis
p. 201 Neal Preston/Corbis
p. 203 Madonna I, 2001 by Andreas
Gursky/SIAE 2011, c-print, 281 x 206 cm
(framed). Courtesy Sprüth Magers Berlin London
p. 204 UPI/eyevine
p. 205 Richard Young/Camera Press
p. 206–7 Vegas5/Camera Press
p. 209 George Rose/Getty Images
p. 210 © Anton Corbijn
p. 212 Neal Preston/Corbis
p. 213 (above left) Blank Archives/
Getty Images
(above right) Jacky Naegelen/Reuters

(below right) Jason Bell/Camera Press
p. 215 MGM/Album
p. 217 Hervé Gloaguen/Gamma-Rapho
p. 219 Bob Seidemann
p. 220 Terry Smith/Camera Press
p. 221 Bob Gruen/www.bobgruen.com
p. 223 Albert Watson
p. 224–25 Guido Harari/Contrasto
p. 227 Patti Smith, 1978 by Robert Mapplethorpe
© The Robert Mapplethorpe Foundation.
Courtesy Art+Commerce
p. 228–29 Brian Aris
p. 231 Annie Leibovitz/Contact Press Images/
LUZphoto
p. 232 Mary McCartney/Camera Press
p. 233 Miramax/Everett Collection
p. 234 Jiri Rezac/eyevine
p. 235 Michel Linssen/Getty Images
p. 237 © Anton Corbijn
p. 238 Guido Harari/Contrasto
p. 239 Guido Harari/Contrasto
p. 240–41 Neal Preston/Corbis
p. 243 Marco Grob/Trunk Archive
p. 244 Guido Harari/Contrasto
p. 246 Dennis Morris/Camera Press
p. 247 (above left) Philip Jones Griffiths/
Magnum Photos
(above right) Enrico Bossan/Contrasto
(below right) Guy Le Querrec/
Magnum Photos
p. 248–49 Gilles Peress/Magnum Photos
p. 251 Phil Stern
p. 252 Phil Stern
p. 253 David Steen/Camera Press
p. 255 Andre Sas/Gamma-Rapho
p. 256 Bob Campbell/Corbis
p. 257 Henry Diltz/Corbis
p. 258–59 Kevin Cummins/Getty Images
p. 261 Guy Le Querrec/Magnum Photos
p. 262–63 Neal Preston/Corbis
p. 265 Dennis Stock/Magnum Photos
p. 266 Elliott Landy/Magnum Photos

p. 267 Elliott Landy/Magnum Photos

p. 268–69 Paul Postle/Camera Press

p. 270–71 Paramount Pictures/Album

p. 272 Efrem Raimondi/Contrasto

p. 273 Baatz/Laif

p. 275 Terry O'Neill/Camera Press

p. 276–77 Nicolas Tikhomiroff/Magnum Photos

p. 279 Giuseppe Pino/Contrasto

p. 280–81 Gordon Parks/Time Life Pictures/
Getty Images

p. 282 Guy Le Querrec/Magnum Photos

p. 283 Guy Le Querrec/Magnum Photos

p. 284–85 Neal Preston/Corbis

p. 286–87 Bruce Davidson/Magnum Photos

p. 288 Guido Harari/Contrasto

p. 290 Rota/Camera Press

p. 291 (above left) Theodore Wood/
Camera Press
(above right) Mike Persson/Camera Press
(below right) Nick Wilson/Camera Press

p. 292–93 Keystone Pictures/eyevine

p. 295 Bob Whitaker/Camera Press

p. 297 Albert Watson

p. 299 © Anton Corbijn

p. 300–1 Guido Harari/Contrasto

p. 303 Albert Watson

p. 304–5 David Strick/Redux

p. 307 © Anton Corbijn

p. 309 Guido Harari/Contrasto

p. 310 Tim Mosenfelder/Corbis Sygma

p. 311 Dave M. Benett/Getty Images

p. 312–13 Jim Watson/AFP/Getty Images

p. 315 http://residents.com

p. 317 *Grace Jones, 1984* by Robert Mapplethorpe
© The Robert Mapplethorpe Foundation.
Courtesy Art+Commerce

p. 318 Everett Collection

p. 319 Barry Schultz/Camera Press

p. 321 Archivio GBB/Contrasto

p. 322 Bob Leafe/Corbis

p. 323 Everett Collection

p. 324 Mark Stewart/Camera Press

p. 325 Derrick Santini/Camera Press

p. 326 Lynn Goldsmith/Corbis

p. 328 (above) Giancolombo/Contrasto

p. 329 (above left) Keystone Pictures/
eyevine
(right) Mark Shenley/Camera Press
(below) Terry O'Neill/Camera Press

p. 330 David Corio/Getty Images

p. 331 Dennis Stock/Magnum Photos

p. 332–33 Everett Collection

p. 334 Everett Collection

p. 335 Everett Collection

p. 337 Keystone Pictures/eyevine

p. 338–39 Giuseppe Pino/Contrasto

p. 340–41 Lawrence Schiller/Camera Press

p. 342 Elliott Landt/Magnum Photos

p. 343 Terry O'Neill/Getty Images

p. 345 Nick Wilson/Getty Images

p. 346–47 Alex Agor/Camera Press

p. 348–49 Terry O'Neill/Camera Press

p. 351 Terry O'Neill/Getty Images

p. 352–53 Elliott Landy/Magnum Photos

p. 355 Barry Feinstein © Barry Feinstein
Photography LLC

p. 356 Lynn Goldsmith/Corbis

p. 357 Everett Collection

p. 358–59 Ivan Nagy/Camera Press

p. 361 Frank Dandridge/Camera Press

p. 363 Eve Arnold/Magnum Photos

p. 365 Randolph/Camera Press

p. 366 Vienna Report/Camera Press

p. 367 Sam Falk/Redux

p. 369 Damon Winter/Redux

p. 370 Guy Le Querrec/Magnum Photos

p. 371 Bruno Barbey/Magnum Photos

p. 372–73 Nik Wheeler/Corbis

p. 374 Terry O'Neill/Camera Press

p. 375 Lagarde/Camera Press

p. 376–77 Tony Frank/Corbis

p. 379 David Chancellor/Camera Press

p. 380–81 Jan Persson/Camera Press

p. 382 Herb Ritts © Herb Ritts Foundation

p. 384 Andy Cotterill/CameraPress
p. 385 (left) Bryan Adams/Camera Press
    (above right) Giuseppe Pino/Contrasto
    (below right) Andrew Winning/Reuters
p. 386–87 Album
p. 389 John Loengard/Time Life Pictures/
    Getty Images
p. 390 Baron Wolman
p. 391 Everett Collection
p. 393 Herb Ritts © Herb Ritts Foundation
p. 394 Giuseppe Pino/Contrasto
p. 395 Phil Knott/Camera Press
p. 396 Derrick Santini/Camera Press
p. 397 Giuseppe Cecchetti/Corbis
p. 398 Guido Harari/Contrasto
p. 399 Theo Wargo/Wireimages/Getty Images
p. 401 Guido Harari/Contrasto
p. 402 Claudia Rorarius/eyevine
p. 403 Stephen Chernin/Getty images
p. 404 Giuseppe Pino/Contrasto
p. 405 Giuseppe Pino/Contrasto
p. 407 Wendy Hu/Corbis
p. 409 Herb Ritts © Herb Ritts Foundation
p. 410–11 Tony Frank/Sygma/Corbis
p. 413 UPI/eyevine
p. 414–15 James Veysey/Camera Press
p. 416 Felix Clay/eyevine
p. 418 Keith Bedford/Reuters
p. 419 (left) Vegas5/Camera Press
    (above right) Album
    (below right) Bruce Davidson/
    Magnum Photos
p. 420–21 Dwayne Senior/eyevine
p. 423 Fausto Giaccone/Anzenberger
p. 424 Keystone Pictures/eyevine
p. 425 Central Press/Getty Images
p. 426 Burt Glinn/Magnum Photos
p. 427 Dennis Stock/Magnum Photos
p. 428–29 F. Driggs Collection/Magnum Photos
p. 431 Bruce Davidson/Magnum Photos
p. 432 Chris Steele Perkins/Magnum Photos
p. 433 Guy Le Querrec/Magnum Photos
p. 435 Dennis Morris/Camera Press
p. 436 Thomas Hoepker/Magnum Photos
p. 437 Alyson Aliano/Redux
p. 438–39 Richard Stonehouse/Camera Press
p. 441 Christian Heeb/Laif
p. 442 Dave Young/eyevine
p. 443 Dave Young/eyevine
p. 444 James Veysey/Camera Press
p. 445 Ezio Petersen/eyevine
p. 447 Michael Jackson # 1 by Valérie Belin,
    2003. Courtesy Galerie Jérome-de-Noirmont,
    Parigi
p. 448–49 Chris Steele Perkins/Magnum Photos
p. 451 Keystone/Gamma-Rapho/Getty Images
p. 452–53 Bruno Barbey/Magnum Photos
p. 454 Monika Graff/eyevine
p. 455 SUS/Camera Press
p. 456 Igor Starkov/Anzenberger
p. 457 Richard Stonehouse/Camera Press
p. 459 David Giles/Camera Press
p. 460 Walter Bibikow/Age Fotostock
p. 461 Walter Bibikow/Age Fotostock
p. 462–63 Stephen Shaver/IPI/eyevine
p. 464 Tania Russo
p. 470 Gil Cohen Magen/Reuters
p. 474 Hulton Archive/Getty Images